Where is your strength?

BY

LAWUNMI A NWAIWU

Copyright

WHERE IS YOUR STRENGTH?

Published by Golden Aisle Weddings 2020

Copyright © 2020 by Lawunmi A Nwaiwu

ISBN 978-0-9933503-2-0

Printed in the United Kingdom

First Edition: June 2020

Published by Golden Aisle Weddings

Dedication

This book is dedicated to anyone who wishes to take control of their life, to discover their unique strengths and to reach their full potential and lead the life they want to live.

I have written this book for you, to guide and help you refill your reservoir of strength, motivation and hope for possibilities to live a better life.

Table of Contents

Preface

Lawunmi Nwaiwu prefaces *Where is your Strength?*, *a journey* she thought she had all figured out.

All the career aspirations and life goals she had planned, only to face a reality full of surprises in her early 20s. She self-reflects on her growth and development on career choices and life decisions made, transitioning from childhood to adulthood, and how her thinking has evolved. In a short statement, she says, "I appreciate the moral principles and values which have shaped me into who I am today. It has been an important part of discovering my true identity and that is why today, I am finally doing the things that resonate with my gifts and values to live a fulfilling life".

In writing *Where is your Strength?*, she notes to readers that although she had numerous goals and milestones she expected to reach at certain points in my life, like so many others, she was often left disappointed when things didn't go according to plan but she kept walking in faith, believing that eventually there will be a breakthrough. She says, "I needed to understand that expectations don't always match reality. It was a challenging but interesting phase in my life which felt perfect sharing with others that it's okay if things aren't happening on your planned schedule. Your milestones may be delayed but if you keep walking in faith, they will surely be achieved and some may even come in unexpected forms".

Some chapters were written based on her self-reflection to past memories - her childhood upbringing while reminiscing with key family members on certain events that had happened which also helped in bringing back those refreshing and life-significant experiences that have shaped her values today.

With the help of her mother, she was able to gather some interesting facts about her relocation from Nigeria to the UK as a teenager, adapting to a different culture and embracing a new chapter of her life. She shares some old photos with readers in the first few chapters, from childhood to adulthood which has triggered some good memories - with friends, loved ones and most especially those that have positively influenced her and contributed to the story she shares today.

During the writing process, she seeks inspiration from other writers on Medium, motivational speakers like Iyanla Vanzant and everywhere to keep her creative mind on alert - in the shower, after breakfast, while driving, listening to music, or while taking care of her home. In order to discover her true identity, she finds inspiration within, drawing the feeling from different situations or activities and begins to appreciate her perseverance in faith and the constant prayers, regardless of the past disappointments, failures, or delay she experienced.

She adds, "It was an emotional journey of self-exploration writing some chapters, most especially *fighting temptations, losing it all, gaining much more* and *the superwoman in you - career, marriage and motherhood*, because these were testing times in her life that she began to discover her inner strength". Today, she's a strong, driven, brave and dependable woman who turned her pain into power. All she feels now is a surge of acceptance and gratitude for those experiences and the new things she has learnt.

She thanks her family, her mentors, the inspirational teachings by Pastor David Sola Oludoyi of Royal Connections and Systems for Living book author, Pastor David Adabale of New Wine Church which has helped her to redefine her life towards happiness and also to live her life in and on purpose.

She hopes this book will encourage and empower anyone who wishes to take control of their life, to reach their full potential and lead the life they want to live. This book prepares and equips them with thoughtful and unique tips on discovering their inner strength during life's challenges.

Introduction

Can you recall the last time you faced a setback or an obstacle that really questioned your purpose in life?

Many times, you may not realise your strengths until you find yourself in situations or challenges that make you feel all hope is lost and you stop believing that something you want to happen might be possible. It happens! Most of us have all been there - but how was I able to mentally recover from setbacks in life?

I experienced a setback many years ago that left me financially exhausted which was one of the hardest and darkest times in my life. It was a struggle to have a penny to my name, but growing up, I began to appreciate the life lessons learnt through my journey. Life challenges can test our faith, patience and inner strength and while these tough times can be hard, *Where is your Strength?* will provide definitive ways to successfully deal with them.

Overcoming the challenges of getting my desired career job after graduation, redirecting my career to incorporate what truly excites me, dealing with redundancy during my pregnancy, overcoming self-doubt, and cultivating habits to develop for financial stability and success have helped me discover the fire within. I realised that I am much stronger than I thought and that I have the faith to continue fighting and not give up. We cannot escape challenges but we can choose how to respond to them and by building up your inner strength, it will unleash your full potential to make the impact you want, become productive, more engaged and have greater joy in the work and life that you truly deserve.

Where is your Strength? will guide you on a journey of self-discovery to think about and realise yourself. We all have expectations and goals. Some people prioritise career over personal life milestones. That was the life I believed in my 20s - I was ready for a life focused on my job first and relationships second. Some of us get married in our late 20s, some do much earlier, and while others don't get married until their late 30s or 40s, it is okay. We're all on different paths and there's no point in comparing your life with anyone else's. It doesn't mean you have failed and you just have to accept that the path you are actually on is important.

Life may look so dim and lonely during the difficult times in your life. With different voices in your head all at the same time. With the loud noises speaking fear, uncertainty and doubt. Where can you find courage when you keep fighting every day and wonder when will all the struggle end?

Where is Your Strength? uncovers some truths about life and learning experiences that will help and guide readers to better understand their lives, solve any personal problem, or prevent any aspect of life from getting worse and more importantly, experience life on a whole new level.

20 Years Ago

Reflection on my past

Life lessons learnt in my 20s

Conversation with Lawunmi Nwaiwu

Something to think about

20 years ago

"The best time to plant a tree was 20 years ago. The second best time is now".

-   Chinese proverb

For many of us, we look at the past few years of our lives and wonder how time flies. Looking back, we may have had big dreams, a big picture of where we would see ourselves today, but somehow things haven't worked out as we hoped for.

Most of my childhood was spent in Nigeria, in Lagos mainland with my big mummy and first cousins. Growing up, I remember on every birthday I always had a cake baked and would celebrate with friends either at school or home. It was awesome. Many times, these moments of love filled the void in my heart of not having my mother around throughout my childhood but I always felt her presence through her voice, letters, presents and it made me know she was always with me. Growing up in Nigeria wasn't all fun and games. My family was strict, in a good way though. You couldn't be too careless or too playful and forget your manners. Being the only child of my mom, there were limitations to how much I was exposed to then. All for the good reasons of not getting mixed up with the wrong crowd. I was mostly indoors, so I didn't have many friends, and the few friends I had were from school. There were only a few that were allowed to come and visit me at home and when they come, they would have to leave before it got dark. It's quite funny, right? But it was all part of being disciplined. I

can remember keeping an eye on the clock, making sure they weren't overstaying their welcome; notwithstanding, it didn't discourage them from visiting and we were still able to have some fun and enjoyed having a selection of big mummy's delicious pastries & cakes.

In my childhood in Nigeria, I had the opportunity to receive an education. I remember our class teachers were also strict. We were always expected to be on our best behaviour and be disciplined, and if we got on the wrong side of our teachers for performing poorly in our exams or not participating actively in class, our parents were usually informed and it meant more trouble waiting at home. Therefore, getting below average was not an option! I changed primary school twice. Apparently, my class teacher felt I talked a lot in class! Well... I'd prefer to say I was only trying to be friendly and interactive with my classmates, sharing intellectual views on education, obviously! That gradually changed, I became more reserved. Another time I remember vividly well was when I fell from the school window and landed face-first. I was really playful that day that I forgot its limits. I was rushed to the first aid room. At that moment, I hadn't realised how much blood was on my face or how deep the injury was, not until I was sent home to recover. I was literally scared of walking home, it was just 10minutes walk from school, but this time I walked home almost as if I was counting my steps. I got home and realised how lucky I was to have survived that fall. My flesh had cut so deep that it left a permanent scar. I became so easily identified because of it and was questioned about the scar until my early twenties.

I remember how low my self-esteem was because I became so conscious of the scar. I could feel it becoming my identity. It was the first thing people would get drawn to and would ask questions on how I got the scar. It's funny how the very little things that shouldn't matter to anyone, are the things we let ourselves get upset about. These little things make us feel uncomfortable around others and we'd want to crawl back into our comfort zone and remain hidden. As time went on, I said to myself that my scar is never something to be ashamed of and I no longer paid attention to it.

I went to the UK to continue my secondary school education in a different environment which made me more anxious. I didn't know what to expect and although I had no friends, I felt I was going to adapt just fine. Well, until it got to a point. Have you ever felt that people in a small environment will accept you only if you're someone like them or if you match their standards? The feeling like you don't fit in? Or because you come from a different background with an accent?

I was mimicked, pranked and laughed at because they thought it was funny for the amusement of others. Many times I had suppressed the thoughts of being a bully because I grew up with morals to not get involved in fights. There were school detentions for students with unruly behaviours and I didn't want to be associated with that. But being under the pressure of not retaliating or standing up for myself and was considered weak by my school mates; for not fighting back. There I was, trying to be the good girl, minding my own business, turning the other way, getting my grades and staying focused. I didn't want to attend school every day because I wouldn't have to see any of those girls. I didn't want to feel scared anymore. So I finally plucked up the courage to stand up for myself and I confronted them. That was the moment everything changed - for better.

You may not become the person you imagined you would be after high school. But that's not the end of the world!

During my youth, I never really wanted to go back to Nigeria because of the support for learning made available in the UK. At the same time, being so far from my hometown made me think about what my home state meant to me and how it had also contributed to shaping me into the person I am today. There is no way I can forget where I come from. There's a saying that goes… "There is no place like home".

I graduated from the university with a Bachelor's Degree in Marketing and Business Entrepreneurship and a Master's Degree in International Business and Marketing, even though it wasn't a guarantee of a prestigious job. I wondered to myself, isn't that what a degree was meant to do? You spend your youth getting educated, in the hope that when you emphasise on what you know, you'd get a job? I had hoped that with all the time spent in the university, that I would get that dream job and not just a student loan debt accumulated. I came to understand that a degree just wasn't enough. One would also need to have the practical experience and I would think to myself that how do employers expect fresh graduates to have acquired the level of work experience if they are not even given the chance to prove their skills? And how do I encourage a student who thinks after higher education that they would get their dream job immediately after graduation? I come from an

African origin, where our parents have made us understand that education comes first before anything. I come from a background where we were given strict advice not to get too close to the opposite sex, not to go out late in the night or even think of getting involved in a relationship at a young age. It was expected that we focus on getting high grades in school, bury ourselves in books, get involved in sports and all the other things school have to offer so that we could get the desired career.

Today, looking back at my childhood, I am grateful about my progress so far and how much I have learnt while going through life's experiences because I wouldn't be where I am today without the place I grew up and the morals it taught me. There is nothing wrong in reflecting on the past and reminiscing over a great period of growth in your life. It is good because it will enable you to learn more and also put you in a frame of mind that helps you make sense of your current state, as long as you don't dwell too long on it, and you keep moving forward.

My relationship with my mom wasn't always a smooth ride at first when I came into the UK. We needed to start understanding each other's way of doing things - *living together*. I always admired her strength, courage and desire to give me the best and unconditional love a mother can give her daughter. Her courage and strength were what encouraged me because even when times were difficult for her as a single mother, she kept pressing on and exercised faith through it all. That was why I strived to become a woman who believes in keeping up good courage, so I could come out on top.

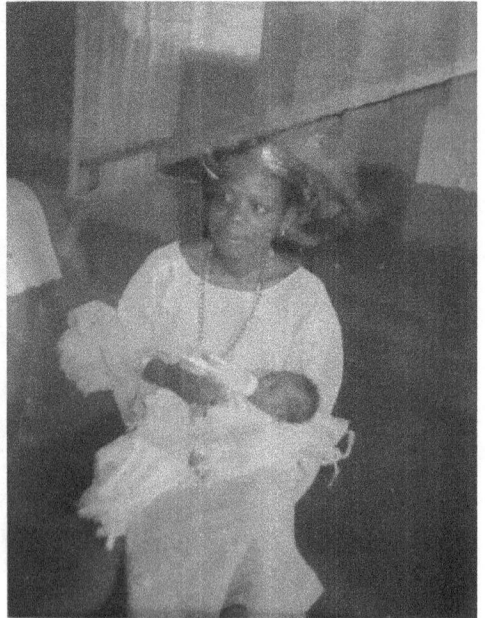

Growing up with my mom; a single parent is special, but it was not easy. What I have learnt throughout my past 20 years in the UK is that a single

parent would do anything in their power to make their children happy and give them the best possible life they can. Being the only daughter of a single mother meant a one-on-one relationship, at times very protective to ensure that I didn't come close to harm, or involved with the wrong crowd. But I knew I'd still be left to make life decisions on what direction I wanted to embark on and remain focused - not forgetting where I came from, especially in an environment where the culture was different.

As I got older, I knew I could depend on her, but I also knew that I needed to start learning independence at a very young age because she was always working long hours to be able to provide for me and didn't really have time to socially mingle with her friends as such. Her time and energy were dedicated to providing for us. Even though I got used to the fact that she couldn't always be there, I became even more adventurous with my entrepreneurial desire. I was more determined to work hard and live the life she always hoped for– be educated, be career-driven, get married and all the rest. *God willing!*

I started experiencing how to be strong on my own, adopting a lot of self-discipline and making sure I was keeping up with my responsibilities. As a result, I became more matured quickly and learnt a few things about growing up that some of my peers didn't learn until much later. Sometimes, watching someone work so hard becomes an inspiration for you to do your absolute best to become better and today, I still think nothing is impossible. I had the mindset to keep pushing for positive results and also keeping the faith that eventually, greater things will begin to happen.

Over the past years, other people also played important roles in my upbringing. My big mummy would attend special parents' days at my school, she also gave me comfort and inspired me to discover my true purpose. I was privileged to have grown up with loved ones around me who have either chipped in, in one

way or the other and cared in their own little way.

Finding one's true purpose is the best part of life and once you find yours, the sky's the limit! The first lesson is to never take anything for granted. These were lessons I learnt from where I grew up and today, I appreciate the moral principles that have come with it. As a result, it has guided and helped me live a life that I can be proud of, which is my desire to use to help others too. While there are many in good health, who have access to the free resources, or can receive help to pursue their dreams but how many actually bother to do the needful? Anything that will bring added value into our lives, let's get right on it. Start looking into things that inspire you because inspiration will spark creativity in YOU. It will help you discover your passion and enable you to start doing amazing things.

Have you ever felt like you haven't received the recognition that you deserve? Felt like you haven't hit your peak yet? These are questions I find interesting reflecting on the past because we all want that valued and appreciated feeling within. It boosts our morale and motivation. So I wondered why I wasn't getting the recognition.

Yes, I would get the small wins but the ones I would have dedicated more time and effort on were overlooked! Staring in the mirror, I would ask myself - is there something I am doing wrong? Is it my attitude that's holding me back? Or maybe my approach towards dealing with a situation? I decided to pay more attention to what I talk about and the comments I make. As well as having a reflection on previous conversations I've had and reviewing how they turned out. I've come to learn over the years that if I continue expecting to receive the appreciation and compliments from others to feel valued, I will be waiting a long time.

You shouldn't have to feel a need for others to acknowledge you to be able to feel your sense of worth and yes, it is possible for you to feel your own sense of value and worth without waiting on others to trigger it. So how did I find value within myself? It started by paying attention to my emotions, which came with knowing all the negative traits and finding a way to work on them, as well as the good traits and finding a way to focus on them more and use them to stand out.

Your motivation starts from within.

You set your own standards of achievement.

Once you set your own standards of achievement, you'd know that you have done a good job without verification from others around you. I started motivating myself internally, knowing that I was going to work hard for my own benefit and self-growth. Of course, I would still love to receive praise and recognition, but I had cultivated self-discipline that I was not going to let it dampen my motivation if I didn't get it. Paying attention to my commitment to work, my attitude, my progress, reviewing previous conversations, and finding ways to improve on learning has led me to being recognised today in some areas of my life. Patience pays off, in the end, they say - when you don't do things for recognition, but because you want to grow. Do things because they resonate with your gifts and values. The feeling of accomplishment comes from within. When you expect others to appreciate what you do, it could lead to you being frustrated that your efforts are not valued.

Conversation with Lawunmi Nwaiwu

Q. 1   You wrote about your struggle to secure a job after graduation. What advice will you give to graduates who need career encouragement?

A. 1   Remain positive. Don't get discouraged when a job you really want does not work out for you. I used it as an opportunity to learn and discover more about myself, so it could lead me to other opportunities. Most importantly, be patient and prepare for the future by gaining knowledge about your desired field - either from professionals or anyone who inspires you and start making connections.

Q. 2   How did the environment you grew up in affect your behaviour? How did it contribute to your personal development?

A. 2   Growing up in Lagos, I lived in a quiet and peaceful neighbourhood, maybe too quiet in fact. However, looking back, I appreciate it more now because it contributed to a safe and healthy life. My cultural values and beliefs have guided me in making life choices in my career and family.

Q. 3   What responsibilities did you have at home when you were young?

A. 3   I am the only child from my mom but I started learning how to do some house chores at an early age - basic cooking, washing dishes, light cleaning and tidying which I surprisingly enjoyed doing and has also contributed to my growth as a woman.

~ **Something to think about** ~

1. Find a quiet and comfortable space where you can sit down and be uninterrupted for at least an hour.

2. Have a pen, paper and a cup of tea or something.

3. Take a few minutes to reflect on the past.

4. Ask yourself about the experiences that brought you happiness in the past. Consider everything from big achievements to smaller special moments.

5. What were some of your biggest struggles or worries in the past?

6. What do you want to continue doing that will move you closer to a feeling of greater happiness, peace and purpose?

The key is that we define ourselves by what we have learnt over the past years and the people who have helped shape us into who we are today. We become a product of maturity and lessons learnt which has given us the strength we need to overcome obstacles that can hinder our growth. Let's constantly strive to grow so that even if we reminisce on our past, we can say our past wasn't our best. Let's challenge the old assumptions of self-growth and find new opportunities that open our creative minds and bring nothing but joy to our lives.

Growing into Yourself

Becoming more of yourself

Reigniting your passion for life

Living in the present for the future

Conversation with Lawunmi Nwaiwu

Something to think about

Growing into Yourself

"The only journey is the journey within".

- Rainer Maria Rilke

Where am I going with my life? Is a question I asked myself some years ago. "I really need to make myself an action plan", I muttered silently.

Growing up, acceptance was probably the most valuable lesson I learnt. Accepting my mistakes, shortcomings, wrong decisions and failures. No matter how many decisions or actions I made in the past that I am not entirely proud of, I've come to realise that everything happens for a reason. Not having that dream job immediately after graduation, there was a reason! Taking a gap year to go on a work internship in a different country, there was a reason! Losing a court case, there was a reason! Why I grew up with a single parent, there was a reason! Why I might have helped the wrong people, there was a reason! In all, I accepted my past, because my past and all the things I have learnt has turned me into a matured woman and also helped to understand, process and move on to live with an empowered mindset, in preparation for whatever hurdle that came by. That is why today, I never regret the decisions I've made, no matter what or where they led me to in life. For those who may have hurt me, disappointed me, or didn't appreciate my efforts, today, I can say I converted the pain into an indomitable spirit that powers the fire inside me each day. I refused to give up on my destiny to succeed in life. I believe that everyone wants to live a fulfilling and great life. Nobody wants to go downhill, feeling depressed or living life feeling constantly stuck. That's why you need to grow continually to live a better life from your present state. It does not stop until you live a fulfilled life.

Every small progress is still a progress

I've always embraced change, even when I haven't thought everything through. In today's world, things are changing so rapidly that it has become important to stay up-to-date with digital trends and keep improving in every area of our lives. Many times I have taken risks in everyday life, but it was in doing so that I was able to determine what works and what does not. I've always had the desire of owning a business. I wasn't entirely sure what the service or product would be, but I knew within me that I would someday manage my own business. Going on an internship meant experiencing a new environment and a different working culture. Although I never had a clear idea of what I wanted, I had an open mind that I would find the answer there. I came to understand that I needed to rectify my steps in pursuing my dreams and also start setting clear goals. So I went back to university to complete my three-year Bachelor's Degree course and I also completed a Master's Degree programme as well. Initially, few friends who we had graduated together thought that it might be a waste of time acquiring a master's degree without getting practical experience in the real world but I still wanted to do it, to get that real sense of self-fulfilment and self-satisfaction.

When you start comparing your life to others, you may begin to misplace the purpose and direction of just being you. Your friends and yourself may have all started together but you all have different destinies. Don't be discouraged if you see that few of your childhood friends are working in prestigious companies, or successful in their respective businesses and you are not there yet, your own time will come. Just keep pushing forward. This could also happen in your line of work. While working with individuals in leadership positions who were much younger than I was, I started feeling self-doubt at work, assuming that I wasn't good enough for the job. I found myself gradually taking the back seat in responsibilities, losing motivation - thinking my opinion was not worthwhile.

On many occasions, my colleagues would win awards in their respective roles and I'd wonder when my time would come or what was wrong with my performance. By recognising that I was having self-doubt at work, it encouraged me to take actions to fix it. I decided to talk to my supervisor about my concerns and I also made plans to start taking on responsibilities that brought me more satisfaction - whether or not I was recognised for my performance. That bit of self-doubt made the experience much more enlightening and challenging; putting me in a healthier position to assess my career goals and refresh how they align with my strengths. I was motivated to keep learning and continue growing; acquiring the skills that would make me better.

Do you ever feel like you are taking a giant step forward, but suddenly it feels like you've hit a roadblock and back to square one? Question yourself on what you are doing or where you are going? Where will your life be in the next five or ten years if you continue doing what you are doing today?

Over time, I formed a habit of asking myself some of these questions all the time and there is absolutely nothing wrong in doing so. I find it helpful because sometimes we just need to take a break for a minute, to examine the kind of life we are living so that we can unlock our full potential and achieve our greatest dream.

I practised a few steps that have helped me to grow in life, but first I would like you to take a moment to think about how far you have come? Looking back to 5 years ago, do you feel you are reaching your life goals? At present, do you feel you are living your dreams? Once you have thought these through, let's look at the steps that guide you back on the right track of growth. Here are 5 steps you can take to help you grow in life:

1. **Commit to taking baby steps:** Every little step taken brings you closer to living the life you've always wanted. Decide on what you want to improve, whether it is your time management skills, relationships, your lifestyle, your parenting skills, or your business acumen etc. Take things one step at a time. If you try to address everything too fast, they may become overwhelming and frustrating, especially if you are not seeing the improvements expected. So focus on building your self-confidence. Improve one thing at a time and build your momentum gradually.

2. **Look at how you live your life:** Make a list of things that are preventing you from living the life that you want. Is it your working hours? Is it your responsibility at home? Or do you find yourself worrying a lot about issues you are currently facing that's hindering your growth? You can begin your new journey by writing down 3 or 4 top priority goals in your life and start working towards them.

3. **Create your own opportunities:** You can wait for opportunities to come by or you can get out there and create your own. Be committed to your growth. Take courses. Self-reflect. Build on your strengths. Review your purpose once every 3-6 months or whichever method that works for you, so that you can know you're on the right path.

4. **Learn from criticism:** Be open to critics but don't be affected by it. Criticism is meant to help you be a better person. Asking for feedback gives us an added perspective about ourselves. Some people you could consider approaching are friends, family, colleagues, your boss, or even acquaintances. If you find that you are always wanting things a certain way with other people, and it's affecting or putting a strain on your relationships, then maybe it's time to take some time to reassess and let go of the obsession of having things done in a certain way.

5. **Let go of relationships that do not serve you:** That means negative people, dishonest people, people who don't respect you, people who are overly critical, and relationships that prevent you from growing. Get out there and make new friends — whether at your workplace, online, or in social groups. Surround yourself with people who also want the best in you.

I cultivated the habit of getting tasks done before the deadline. Whenever I have meetings with prospective clients, I prepare notes in advance on any questions that may arise and I remind myself on why my meeting will be a phenomenal success. Some of my friends would say I have a serious and professional approach. Well, I guess so but this is what comes with having an entrepreneurial mindset. You want to win! Especially when you know you are the only one that can drive your passion, and get your business growing to the level you want.

1.1 You are not lost! Bring out the brighter you

1. **Pay more attention to yourself:** Start by finding the right direction in your life - focusing on your greatness. You are the only one who can determine which direction your life is going to take because you will be the one to take the steps to realise your path.

2. **Speak life into your life:** Tell yourself positive things about who you want to be. I gradually became the woman who believed in her right to be here… A woman who feels she can make a difference… A woman who feels bold and courageous to be different… And I would tell myself daily, I am blessed! I will continue to move forward! I am getting stronger and by faith, I will continue to open doors of breakthrough in my life! When you truly believe the good declarations upon your life, it will begin to happen; all in God's time.

3. **Remove the negative thoughts:** We will soon come to realise that the better person that we've always dreamed of has always been in there. The sooner we can remove all the negative voices telling us that we cannot be successful, the easier we will be able to move forward. Being you is a powerful energy force to be the highest possible expression of yourself because when you do, you will attract the right people and the right opportunities that you'd never thought in your wildest dreams were possible. You really have to truly engage with your life in order to get anywhere. When you hit roadblocks, be gentle and remember who you are. There will be moments where you might get disappointed, heartbroken, or make rational decisions that you might regret or be confused about what to do next; but remember, you are not lost! If you're constantly asking yourself where your choices are taking you and if you're making the right ones, you're not alone!

When I decided to start a career as a wedding planner, it seemed I had everything all mapped out but the problem was where do I start from? I've got all these big dreams but how do I start putting the pieces together. So, I started doing more research, that way I could figure out exactly what would make my business different. Knowing a lot of popular names in the wedding industry, I became stuck on why people would patronise my business - a start-up business for that matter.

No matter how scary and competitive the market is; understanding your competitors and what they are offering is a starting point to defining what your Unique Selling Proposition (USP) is. It will help you decide on how best to market your product or services. It will enable you to set your prices competitively and help you to respond to rival marketing campaigns with your own initiatives.

1.2 You are not lost! Find your path

Sometimes we doubt the direction we are going or may not realise the changes we need to make within ourselves. Many of us need encouragement to begin that change. Some get side-tracked along the way which makes the whole purpose of change become forgotten. But by encouraging the self-confidence and determination in us, we can get to the root of the problem and start making impactful decisions. During a difficult time in my life, I felt that things were not progressing as planned. I was feeling further away from my goals, and I no longer knew the next step to take. If you're like me, you might come to a point where you feel like you've tried everything, and nothing seems to be working; but maybe you just need a different approach. When life doesn't turn out the way we'd hoped, planned, or expected, we feel tremendous disappointment and start doubting everything, including ourselves. Maybe you thought you'd be married by now, but you aren't even dating anyone. Maybe you poured your heart into a project or relationship only to get fired or break up. I'll encourage you that whatever the situation may be, always maintain your cool, take a deep breath, and tell yourself everything will be okay.

It's normal to feel lost at some point, but it is important to remember to pull yourself out of that lonely place of self-doubt, sooner rather than later. I believe breaking points, if well managed, can lead you back into the light, where you can refocus and rebuild your confidence. That will be your starting point to taking those very little steps today, then tomorrow and the next. Gradually, you will begin to notice a change in your attitude, a change in your mindset, and the way you approach different situations. Your steps will get bigger and better, and you will be less tolerant of anyone who is telling you any different from what you believe in. When I officially launched my wedding planning business in 2013, I was finally taking the little steps to bring me closer each day to my dream. The self-confidence in me wasn't just about being better or being different but it was more of seeing myself for all that I have and believing in that. Believing that it will be a positive outcome as things progressed. It was difficult and challenging, but with perseverance and consistency, I finally had a breakthrough. The important part is to never lose motivation and trust that whatever you do today will take you a step closer to what you want to become tomorrow. After getting my first client, I realised that I was actually better than I thought… I had more confidence in my skills. It was just a matter of discovering, learning and understanding my strengths, so I could use them in the right way to achieve real goals.

1.3 You are not lost! Progress starts by doing something

Start doing a lot of the "small things" because they lead to bigger things and better results. The doubts that have held you back will gradually begin to disappear, giving room for more clarity and direction.

1. **Start living the way you want to be remembered:** Be authentic by being focused, dependable and trustworthy in the way you live your life. Start making a positive impact on peoples' lives. I hope to have helped inspire other women to find the strength within even during their trials and tribulations. Helping each other understand that we can make it through anything and not give up. With perseverance, we pray for wisdom in dealing with difficult situations and the patience to be able to stand strong. We can be who we want to be and we would only be hurting ourselves by limiting ourselves.

2. **There is power in staying resilient:** Even when everything seems to be knocking you down. I believe that by making time to invest in myself every day, working harder on myself, I gradually became more skilled and more valuable. When you take time to discover your talents, refine your skills and abilities, you're investing in something that you will always have and nobody can take from you - and as a result, you can add more value to other people.

3. **Don't be afraid to fail:** Despite my new responsibilities as a wife and mother, I still try to create time for myself - to keep working on projects I enjoy doing. I've had failed ideas in the past, but I have learnt some important lessons from them because when we fail, we learn, grow in maturity, and achieve new perspectives on life, love, business, money and relationships. Through each failure in my life, my values were reshaped. What I valued 10 years ago doesn't have the same values today. The values I had in business, finance and relationships are totally different today because I needed to learn to value the right things. When it comes to relationships, I have a smaller circle of friends now but back in high school or university, I had a wider group of friends and would find myself wanting to fit in to please their way of lifestyle. There are still a few I keep in touch with, while there are others who have in one way or the other inspired me in different areas in my life.

4. **Know who you are:** When you lose a sense of who you are; sometimes it can lead to anger or frustration. Do you know why you might be feeling lost? Sometimes it happens if you are letting yourself be controlled by the opinions of others, society, or family on what you are supposed to be doing rather than what you want to be doing. What do you truly desire? If you want to do something great in life, you shouldn't be living under someone else's expectations. It is important to find yourself by figuring out what truly makes you happy. What truly makes you happy will be the drive to open up your potentials to accomplish anything you set your mind to.

Other people may not understand or care about the new path you are on; they may not believe in your ambitions or the life-changing decisions you are about to make; but if you can feel true happiness brewing within and also feel the positive energy it brings, continue believing in yourself. People will begin to believe in you as time goes on. Do more of what you love. Don't hang on to that job that does not fulfil you in any passionate way. I was dedicating 8 hours every day of my time to a company that was not fulfilling my career dream. That doesn't mean I left the job. I simply started running a business so that I could get a real sense of fulfilment, doing what I love and enjoy most.

Whether you have lost yourself in your relationship, job, your health, as a parent, or in anything generally, you are not alone. For some of us, we have been there and it doesn't mean that your life is doomed or that you will never find yourself again; because you will.

Conversation with Lawunmi Nwaiwu

Q. 1 You wrote about your inner struggle with self-confidence and discovering your true identity. How did you know when you found yourself?

A. 1 You will begin to feel a real sense of fulfilment with your passion in life. When you find yourself listening to your gut instincts, believing in yourself, and paying closer attention to your feelings, you'll become a different and better person than who you used to be, and start doing things for yourself instead of for others.

Q. 2 What is different about growing up today from when you were growing up?

A. 2 For one to be mature and wise, you must first have done some young or stupid things at some point in life. The responsibilities that come with being an adult, paying bills, making independent decisions, and taking responsibility for your actions. I've become more matured and responsible in my approach to certain situations. My inner strength which developed throughout my journey via the trials and lessons experienced.

Q. 3 You wrote about going on an internship, a different environment to explore your career. What advice can you give young aspiring individuals who are yet to discover their career path?

A. 3   Have an open mind to change and try new things but you need to start the work first. Take some time to explore careers and see which one you feel most connected with. I did various jobs in retail, clinic, restaurant, customer services, and sales in my early years before I discovered my true passion. It starts by networking and establishing relationships with working professionals which will prepare you for what to expect in your field and increase confidence in your work.

Q. 4   At a point in your life, you needed clarity on your true calling and passion. How did you decide what you wanted to do with your life? How do you feel about that choice?

A. 4   Working in various jobs that I didn't enjoy made me realise my true calling as a wedding planner - not that I regret doing any of these jobs because they also contributed to the skills I have today. There's no certain age to have figured out your passion and there's no protocol on how to but by trying out different things you gain more experience and it makes you understand what you like and don't like. I was inspired by a few business leaders in the industry and watching some real-life business TV shows helped me refocus on my strengths to making small decisions and taking action on my passion without the fear of failing. You wouldn't really know what works best for you not until you have a taste of the experience, and today, these are lessons life has taught me on the journey to discovering my purpose in life.

~ Something to think about ~

Let's see how you get on with few steps to guide you to knowing and loving yourself every day:

1. Love yourself - look at the mirror and tell yourself nice things about you

2. Treat yourself - take a break or a day off and focus on doing a hobby you love, something relaxing or fun

3. Find a comfortable space and start having a growth mindset

4. What areas in your life do you need to change?

5. Decide on how you want to track your progress

Fighting Temptations

Facing the storms of life

Knowing your safe place

Discovering your strengths in the struggles

Conversation with Lawunmi Nwaiwu

Something to think about

Fighting Temptations

"Every moment of resistance to temptation is a victory".

- **Frederick William Faber**

We all face different storms in life. Some are more difficult than others, but we all go through trials and tribulation at some point and the strength to overcome them requires focus and drive to win. Some situations will utterly test our patience, question your judgment on what is right from wrong, and temptations that may doubt your faith. It can happen anywhere, in any area of our lives. It could be at work, marriage, family, education, or in our day to day activities.

Before rededicating my life to God, my youth life had its challenges. Being exposed to the way of the world and suppressing the urge to sin from the influence of peer pressure, in relationships, spiritual growth, career and media. Sometimes, one may desire to do the right things but may be faced with bad situations that could challenge our judgement. Pressure from others can stir up desires in our hearts which could lead to a tempting situation. I feel grateful to have a religious upbringing with biblical teachings that contributes to a wide range of health and well-being outcomes later in life. But without personally having a conviction - a firm belief, it can be a struggle to overcome the storms in life.

Wanting to feel accepted

During my fresher's week at the university, I encountered my first adversity. Generally wanting to fit in, be accepted and appreciated. In other words, basically "being cool". I couldn't possibly have known what it would be like to be away from my family for a long extended time.

In the beginning, most especially in the first academic year, it is expected to feel energized and ready to take on whatever you want, enjoy the social nightlife or possibly take an interest in what you'd usually not attach yourself with when around family. I would ask myself what if this was the way of discovering more about myself? Knowing who you are? Or finding where you belong? Sometimes the question we struggle to answer honestly is if it's really worth it - living a reckless life? Doing so just to be accepted? To receive attention? Or because we are afraid of the perception people may have about us for being different? Many of us convince ourselves of our wrongful thoughts with the - *you only live once* mentality.

I loved listening to music, whether it was in church, in a club, or my room; music kept me going. There wasn't any song back then that I mostly wouldn't know the lyrics to and I would have a dance choreography for my favourites. Who knows, maybe I missed my calling to be a music artist or choir leader during my youth. But where I'm going with this is; having a religious upbringing, how do you then filter out the afrobeats, hip-hop and RnB to stay connected to gospel music or how the media influences society. Growing up in today's world can be complicated. Most especially with the presence and intensity of media influences - television, radio, music, computers, films, videos and the Internet.

My Youth

I remember during my youth, the morning after getting home from a girl's night out, I would hear that little voice in my head asking me if I felt satisfied with my lifestyle. I'd give myself the talk that *"well I go to church, even though I'm not a regular member, but I am still a Christian, I am not involved in worldly behaviours to the extent of others, then I guess I'm just trying to be happy while still young".* The shocking part was I was familiar with a reading in *Ecclesiastes 11:9* that as much as we want to enjoy our youth, and follow our heart desires, we should also *"remember that God is going to judge us for whatever we do".* As we live our daily lives, we may try to convince ourselves that we are not doing anything bad, but if it is not pleasing in the eyes of God, then it should be a wakeup call for us to change our ways. And there I was! Re-evaluating myself, my actions and my lifestyle. I was a little upset emotionally and I thought to myself to give it time that it will pass and I could revisit this part when I'm much older but honestly? I started to grasp the reality of things and realised that if I didn't start being true to myself, I may lose myself in the process.

I learnt the hard way from the situations I've experienced. Some setbacks I encountered brought me back to God, and that decision helped me to avoid peer pressure or social experience tempt me into compromising my standards. Once you stay true to what you believe in, others will respect you more for it. The more you understand your beliefs, the easier it is to hold fast to them and resist any temptation that is contrary to them. It takes time and experience to be able to know your own convictions to avoid the kind of pressure temptation brings. We all experience temptation almost every day of our lives. We may feel that we are strong, but it is not by our own strength that gives victory, but our faith that sees us through. During my youth, I'd say it was the season I struggled most with temptation; a transition into the world of adulthood to establish my identity. It was a process of growth and development which involved a lot of decision making and choices. Therefore, the ability to go through the journey of self-exploration, to find my true identity at a younger age prevented me from risky behaviours today.

Moments of Weakness

Knowing my weaknesses and being honest with myself on what temptations I could be most vulnerable to, prepared me emotionally, spiritually and physically on how to fight them. It is important to understand what you are most vulnerable to. You could start by listing these weaknesses and what you can do to fight it so that the next time you face the temptation you will know how best to deal with it.

I have come to understand that temptation is always conscious. We can't be tempted without the thought first coming into our minds, and so by giving in, knowing full well it is a wrongdoing, it becomes a sin. A temptation may last long but the most important thing is that you do not stop fighting it. Whether it is anger, stealing or whatever you may be struggling with personally, continue resisting until the urge is dead.

Many years ago, I noticed doing the right thing made me lose a couple of friends. Even though I may have felt I needed a lot of friends, to feel a sense of belonging, I soon started to realise that if I truly wanted to focus on improving myself, at some point I would need to outgrow certain friends. We need to be around friends that will share an interest in your work.

You don't need a lot of friends in your life. Just the right ones.

To the Point of Passion

Even in romantic relationships, many of us struggle with the pressure of being physically involved or having to keep reassuring our partner of our feelings without having any physical intimacy. Today, many ask, can a relationship survive without any intimacy? It happens that physical intimacy can be more important to one partner than the other - where one may be more emotionally involved and the other may be more physically involved. So when they both find themselves getting along well, thinking everything is fine until one of them finally speaks up and lets the other know that the intimacy level is not where they should be - that becomes the tricky part! What do you do or how do you now respond to the situation without going against your beliefs?

From time to time, I reflect on myself and I realise that the few things that were temptations in my past relationships reassure me now that I was actually better off avoiding them. It's difficult! Especially in those moments, but it pays off in the long run and for the right reasons. I can truly say it was all worth it in the end. Having cultural and religious views of marriage before pregnancy prevented me from wanting to have a baby out of wedlock or going on a journey I knew deeply I was not prepared for. We all have different views on relationships and I am not here to tell you how to manage yours. Rather, I am sharing my personal experience on the choices I made that have led me to where I am today. I believe that you'd know what you want; when you ask yourself what hasn't worked in the past, have a reflection on what kind of relationship you've always imagined and what would make you happy in the long run. I've always wanted to get married before committing to starting a family. I didn't want to be faced with a dilemma or the uncertainties of 'what-ifs' - What if he leaves me? What if we are not ready for the responsibilities? And when it's starting to sound like a lot of what-ifs already, I'd ask myself these key questions - Will I feel better of myself in the long run? Is it really worth it? No! That was the moment I started taking control of my thoughts and avoided putting myself in any situation I knew I may not be able to cope with. The decisions we make today will determine the stories we will tell tomorrow. The bottom line is that you are not in the passenger's seat when it comes to how you deal with temptations. Being in the driver's seat means you let the temptations know who's boss in any situation.

The decisions we make today will determine the stories we will tell tomorrow

---

Not getting what you want

There were some decisions that I have made in the past that turned out to be the wrong decisions. It happens! And I learnt from my mistakes. I wasn't going to live a life taking certain decisions just to please others or in a way that I have to compromise my beliefs, standards and self-respect. There are also some temptations that even despite our best efforts, the flesh is weak and gives in to temptation. We shouldn't quit trying! You may fall a few times, but if you keep trying to strengthen your resolve, you will eventually be able to resist totally. I've come to understand that when people are aware of what you stand for; you tend to attract less of the things that take you out of character. Each one of us has certain habits that are particularly troubling to us.

When I didn't immediately get my dream job after completing my masters, I can recall feeling disheartened. I was discouraged because after acquiring two degrees, I still couldn't get a job with it due to lack of experience and I thought - what was the whole point of getting educated to the master's level? I had friends who didn't even further their education and yet they were getting the best jobs. Some didn't even study at all and yet were successful. Whilst others who didn't have to work so hard moving up the ladder at work. I didn't imagine starting my career at an entry-level and was tempted by thoughts of making quick cash, taking the quickest route. It was quite frustrating because as much as I didn't want to engage myself in such, the 9 to 5 job of a minimum wage wasn't encouraging either. It becomes hard to keep the faith and strength to endure a bit longer especially when you are surrounded by obstacles and situations that feel beyond your control. Notwithstanding, I was determined to continue walking the difficult road, in the hope that it would be the path to success.

When you start putting full trust in yourself and following your intuition, focusing on what you are trying to achieve, you will find yourself moving forward one step at a time with hope and confidence in the future - even during life's setbacks. Some years back, a situation I went through broke me financially. I was full of anger and resentment, but I gradually came to learn that setbacks are a form of practice. Sometimes things have to go wrong for it to go right for you. If I didn't experience such a setback, I probably wouldn't have learnt how to grow through the struggle. I wasn't ready to give up on me, I needed to believe in myself to be able to get back up on my feet. Even though I felt defeated emotionally, I knew it wasn't over for me; and rather than be led astray by the worldly things, I focused on staying true to the path that felt right. Four things that have helped me avoid temptation are:

1. Understanding my weaknesses

2. Not getting discouraged by the flaws

3. Confessing and repenting

4. Praying

For whatever struggle that you may be going through, just know people have also passed through a similar struggle and some people are facing it right now. You are certainly not alone in your struggle.

Feeling unappreciated

Temptation can come through feeling unappreciated and it can change your attitude. Many of us at some point in our lives may have felt that we keep helping others but we are not getting anything in return. And now you are probably getting to the point where out of frustration, you now want to stop helping people. You are not alone. I remember how much I also struggled with this. When I was in school, I used to help a few of my friends with their coursework but sometimes felt it was taken for granted. For me, to be able to get the grades that I wanted, I had to work twice as hard, reducing the social hangouts, but for some people, they probably didn't even need to sweat it to get the grades. There were times when I was growing up that some of my friends would make a request to which I was in the best position in that present time to assist. I started noticing that whenever I needed help, they were either nowhere to be found, or had excuses that they were busy, or they forgot. Some even made empty promises that they would help. How do you deal with the feeling that your pressing need is not considered important or urgent? The interesting thing about helping others and giving yourself peace of mind, which I learnt, is helping wholeheartedly without expecting nothing in return. What I've come to experience and understand is that when we help people the right way, you get a lot of benefits in life, and it may not necessarily be through the people you already know. It could come from a stranger but our biggest rewards are from God.

Turn your feelings of being unappreciated into confidence

If friends don't value your help, avoid engaging in negative thoughts of not wanting to help others who may genuinely need your help and appreciate you for doing so. Focus on the long-term instead of the short-term. Even though I've been disappointed in the past, I didn't let that change who I am. It is painful when people take your kindness or love for granted or make you feel unimportant, but I've always found comfort in reminding myself that there is a greater reward from above and it is real. It is real because even years after, in unexpected ways, I started experiencing kindness from God through others, even in my darkest of times. He sees all that we do and that is why we shouldn't feel alone.

Today, when I look back at past situations I thought I should have been upset about; I just smile with relief and think to myself, so what if I had changed my behaviour out of anger, disappointment and resentment, what would have become of me? Isn't it possible it could have hindered my growth in Christ? The key here is that, whatever we do, let's do it with all our heart and remember you are not doing it for man, you are doing it for the better you and a better generation ahead. Let's not fall into the temptation of halting our blessings or reward by having a hardened heart to stop helping people but pray for guidance to help the right people.

Conservation with Lawunmi Nwaiwu

Q. 1   During your youth, you struggled with fighting temptations, is there anything you regret today in the hopes that the future generation can avoid them?

A. 1   There may be a few past experiences I may have regrets on and that came with not having enough self-confidence but if I keep having self-blame, I'd probably not have been able to move on to achieve other things. It's more about learning from your mistakes and bouncing back. Don't lose your identity to fall on the wrong path. Having self-discipline helped me to take control of my habits and choices.

Q. 2   On your upbringing, you wrote about your cultural values and beliefs which have helped shape your life. If you could share with your family your most important values, what would you say?

A. 2   Never compromise your beliefs because these are the powers we have in life, it has been an important part of my identity. I've had experiences in the past where I wanted to please people and do things their way to fit into their world until I decided to stop compromising my identity, staying true to myself and being happy.

~ Something to think about ~

If you truly believe that you are on the right track which will eventually lead to the right destination, then you can draw comfort and confidence knowing within yourself that you are still maintaining your values in the right way. Have a moment to ask yourself these questions:

1. What is the potential temptation you struggle with?

2. What will you do when the temptation arises?

3. Are you honest with your resolve?

4. What will be the long-term consequences if you give in to temptation?

Losing it All, Gaining Much More

How do you start life over again when it feels like you've lost everything, especially when you are experiencing an unexpected financial disaster and it seems like there is no way you can recover from the setback? Things may look so bad at that moment, that it might feel like all hope is lost. It happens, most of us have all been there - but how was I able to mentally recover from the setback?

Facing a Financial Disaster

Experiencing a financial setback years ago was one of the hardest and darkest times in my life to the point where I struggled to have 2 pennies to my name. This was just before completing my 3rd year at the university. All my savings and everything I earned was all gone due to a court case which was ongoing for 3 years, but I started appreciating life more, growing up. I realised that what I thought I had lost was nothing compared to what others in different areas of their lives may have lost.

When we have a significant financial loss, it's a time we need to start focusing more on what we have. It starts from somewhere and instead of feeling like I lost everything, I acknowledged the loss and started doing the practical thing - starting all over again. I accepted the reality of my financial situation and started carving out some new financial goals and taking action with the right course.

Mentally recovering from the financial crisis

I am very thankful for my mom who was very supportive with encouragement during that difficult time in my life. Of course, it wasn't easy to get back up on my feet. I was full of anger because of the situation, being in full-time education and yet everything was exhausted, I was finding it difficult to keep up with my rent - living off-campus, amongst other bills. During times like this, it's important for us to get back on track by refocusing our thoughts back on - *what can I do? What resources are there for me to use? How do I reduce costs or lighten the financial burden?*

One of the things I tried not to do was to neglect my bills due date because doing so would only make things worse. What I did was to communicate with the companies and set up a payment arrangement plan from as little as I could afford at that time. Many times all we have to do is pick up the phone for professional support. Many of these companies will offer a sliding scale of fees for you to pay what you can afford until you recover.

I started keeping myself busy, doing things that create happiness and fulfilment to avoid dwelling on what happened or how I would have done things differently. It may take some time to rebound from a financial loss, but remain level-headed and focused to get through the period of misfortune.

Recovering What I Lost

Most of us have areas in our lives where we need a breakthrough. This has taught me that whenever we hit rock bottom in any point of our lives, we shouldn't be too quick to assume that it's the end - or find ourselves questioning our purpose in life.

Through self-reflection on my commitment to faith, I questioned whether I had possibly stopped walking by faith and started trying to figure everything out by sight? Or maybe I was seeking things first? And so I decided to rededicate my life wholeheartedly to my faith, becoming more actively involved and connected. With time, I began to experience restoration in all areas in my life and gradually began to forget all the things I thought I had lost, because now, what I recovered was much more. It made me wiser and it has strengthened me in times of struggles or disappointments. Such setbacks are a reminder that if we continue to walk in faith, we recover so much more than what we felt we had lost. It may be an important part of our journey that we have to go through, to be able to begin to enjoy the great and beautiful things waiting for us.

The Superwoman in You: Career, Marriage and Motherhood

The first year of marriage

Balancing a career, marriage and motherhood

Qualities of a superwoman

Conversation with Lawunmi Nwaiwu

The Superwoman:

Career, Marriage and Motherhood

"The real act of marriage takes place in the heart, not in the ballroom or church or synagogue. It's a choice you make – not just on your wedding day, but over and over again – and that choice is reflected in the way you treat your husband or wife".

-   Barbara De Angelis

Life in the 20s is considered to be a crucial and very critical phase in life that sets the building blocks for the future. It is a phase where most youths are freshly-out of the university and are starting to understand the world around them better and also their personal needs.

Rewinding to when I was 24, after completing my one-year internship, I was in between two worlds of whether I wanted to settle down and get married or start a new career; break out of my comfort zone to explore the world; or focus on building a network in my desired industry. The transition into the real world can be both exhilarating and overwhelming, it's no more a theoretical world of books but real-life scenarios. Taking baby steps in the corporate world and exploring all life has to offer. It's a different ball game when you have to get a grip on your finances and shop smart! As time goes on, you realise that you've finally started to understand your purpose in life to some extent and now you desire much more. Then you find yourself at a crossroad of whether to continue focusing on establishing a career or consider starting a family? Sure, a career is important but family is what we live for, both are priorities, but how do you strike a balance on fulfilling both?

My expectations about my future have varied dramatically through different stages of my life. I always imagined that I would be married at some point by my late 20s, escape to a nice property abroad and start a new refreshed family life. During my early 20s, I had that mindset that staying single while identifying and exploring my career options was more ideal at that stage in my life. I didn't want to rush into any ultimate commitment only to rush back out. I wanted to establish a career for myself and be financially stable. Taking professional risks and failing early in my career meant that I wouldn't be putting anyone else in jeopardy, compared to if I was married and taking risks, I could end up putting my family in a bad position.

However, what I didn't realise back then was that you can still pursue a career and still be open to dating. I noticed I became so comfortable with the benefits of being single while building a career for myself. With years going by, it became obvious that I wasn't giving myself an opportunity to meet a true partner who could join me on the journey and give the added benefits of being in a committed relationship (as a supporter - emotionally and financially). I started thinking hard about my future. I asked myself a few questions, like:

- Will I be disappointed if I have not reached certain milestones throughout my journey?

- Am I feeling lonely?

- Do I desire someone to share my life with?

I think that getting married should be about falling in love and finding someone who compliments you perfectly – not about ticking your criteria boxes or doing so because others close to you are already married and with children. A few of my friends had already started a family in their mid-20s and I was happy for them. Sometimes it's natural to have that odd feeling that you are slipping behind - but I knew that my time will come naturally and in God's perfect time. That didn't mean I folded my arms and expected it to happen magically on its own. I started to open myself up more to suitable dating opportunities while focusing on my career. In doing so, I knew that with time, the right person with good intentions will show up at the right time. I believe that no matter your age, the right partner will always respect you for the kind of person you are, as well as your professional achievements.

So, fast forward to the day it finally came to the four-word question - "will you marry me" and all of a sudden, at that moment, I was filled with excitement and lots of questions racing through my mind - is this really happening? the moment is finally here! Should I say yes already? or maybe make him sweat a little and then blurt out, yes? And right there, sweating and giggling, I said yes! It was an amazing spot. I thought we were all getting together to celebrate his birthday with close friends but it was a twist of the event - the spotlight was on me and it was real.

Finally married, we did it! The big day has come and gone; now ready to start the new journey as a married couple, but where to start? It's alright to freak out a little as a newlywed, because the past few months, you've both been planning your perfect wedding and now you've had a beautiful ceremony with loved ones, received and opened all your wedding presents and here you are, wondering what you are supposed to do next? You may start to feel like you have a lot to do but don't know where to start from. The reality of beginning a new chapter in your life with your partner begins to set in. It's time to start living up to your vows and adapting to the new changes; living with your partner and growing a family for the rest of your life.

A wedding is not just the completion of the engagement, it's the beginning of a new life

---

Surviving the First Year of Marriage

It is common to experience some marital issues with your spouse during the first year of marriage. Once you start living together, you may realise that you have different priorities. All couples argue, but it's the way they argue that determines if their relationship will go the distance. Our first year as newlyweds was what I would call the 'teething period' – a period where we were discovering a lot more about each other. I discovered a few principles that helped us get through our newlywed shock period and most especially because we didn't live together before getting married.

Before we got married, my partner and I attended a premarital counselling session so that we could have a better chance for a stable and satisfying marriage, it really helped prepare for the marriage. We needed to understand each other's qualities better so that we could have a strong healthy relationship. The premarital counselling contributed to what we know today. With the support of the senior pastors (premarital counsellors) in Royal Connections who also shared their experiences in their years of marriage as a couple. Although the classes didn't really dig too deep into our personal lives, a couple of questions that struck me the most are:

- How will you handle your relationships with your families?

- What does spirituality mean to you?

These questions were important to discuss because we both needed to have that conversation to understand between ourselves the boundaries and roles of each of our family members. We needed to learn that we are now on a journey of forming a new family entity. Also, understanding our spirituality was important because this is a guiding force in our lives.

When we finally got married, we had to figure out how to live together with a little compromise. We had never lived together before getting married so there were a lot of things we had to learn to adjust to.

Below are a few points that helped us begin our journey towards a healthy marriage. I hope this guides you to discover how you could both unite as one and build a home you'll both love.

1. Communication is key

It is common for both individuals to have different notions about marriage. Most especially if you have known each other for quite some time, you might assume that your partner should know you well enough to be able to know what you like or don't like.

The first year of marriage is the foundation year to start building healthy communication. I remember during our first year, we would argue over how things should be or how we understood things should be in our own way i.e. during my pregnancy, I expected him to be more involved. I would think he was intentionally not bothered about my pregnancy, but after calmly discussing this issue with him, I realised that he just wasn't aware of certain things he needed to do. It was just new to him, and if I had just shared what

I was expecting from him, then he probably would have taken action in the best possible way to be of support. We had to talk to each other about what I was expecting him to do instead of waiting for him to figure it out. By explaining your needs and issues clearly to each other, no matter how many times, it helps strengthen a relationship.

2. Let it go

During our first year together I had to learn to let go of a lot of things. There were little things I had to overlook, we had different approaches to how things were done. Letting the little things annoy us in a big way can also be eating away our relationships. I decided to let go of a lot of things that didn't really matter, mostly the small annoying things my partner would do. By letting little things slide without getting myself overly worked up, or getting easily irritated by his behaviour, I had to learn to accept the things I cannot change about my partner and just focus on improving myself. It's not easy but I decided that rather than creating conflict over little things, it's best to give the benefit of the doubt and just assume they are doing their best.

3. Set a routine

As a newlywed couple, it is important to find a routine that suits both of you. I and my husband both own a business which could at times be hectic for both of us. Due to our different schedules, we were unable to spend quality time together and so after some discussion, we decided to schedule a weekend in a month to either hang out, cook together, watch football, or discuss family goals. That way, we were both having a bit of quality time together, while supporting each other's business. Having a routine that meets all our needs is sometimes hard, but once you are both able to discuss your needs and find a way to make things work together, it helps reduce the strain on your relationship. That doesn't mean you shouldn't create some time for yourself. Sometimes a 'ME' time allows you both to grow as individuals.

4. Enjoy every moment

First-year should be a year for couples to explore things together and have fun, most especially when there are no commitments yet like children.

Remember that a healthy relationship is about letting go, and the willingness to compromise. Now that our home is expanding with more financial responsibilities, we are now mindful of our lifestyle in some areas of our lives.

Before we got married, we'd discussed what our family goals were, our desires and how we would like to work and support each other in our ideal home. It becomes more of a reality when you begin the journey and realise that marriage takes a lot of work and it's not always going to be smooth-sailing.

You can never be sure if a romantic partner is decent enough to marry

---

As a woman, I started discovering more of my strengths and depended solely on the supernatural power of God to become the woman he had called me to be, in every aspect of my life. I started discovering the person I am in Christ and who Christ is in my life. I began to understand how he communicates his word through the Holy Spirit, speaks through other people around me and ordained pastors. Of course, this wasn't always an easy journey for me but since I rededicated my life to God, I gradually learnt more about my natural strengths (and weaknesses) and that I would be helpless without the wisdom from God to be able to withstand the challenges that come in marriage. I knew that no matter how good I might be in some areas of my life, there is a level of excellence that I will not be able to reach on my own strength. When I reflect on how my partner and I started our journey, getting to understand each other, I realised that we needed God more than we'd ever imagined because it wasn't a journey we could have handled with our own wisdom. We needed to keep the faith so that when we meet challenges in life, we would be able to fight together and stand strong in the difficult times.

Who is that Superwoman?

To help and guide me, I have always been inspired by a chapter in the Bible (Proverbs 31). Reading it, I knew I needed to possess those qualities as a woman. It reminded me of the admirable traits I have seen in my mother and other great mothers I know. I saw them as superwomen in the best way they could be. It became part of the reasons why giving up on myself and God wasn't an option. The word 'superwoman' means "a woman who fulfils her many roles, especially one able to do many things well and often, one equally successful in dealing with the demands of work and family". Most women are proud that they can multitask, juggle motherhood with their career and have a great relationship with their partner. However, I've come to understand better that one can become a superwoman by one's own definitions and terms, in a way that one would have a balanced life in content and happiness - without the daily pressure of wanting to do everything but feeling completely exhausted doing so.

The word superwoman in marriage doesn't mean having to be the perfect wife. Playing the perfect wife or trying to prove that you can do it all will probably break you and that is why by passionately doing the best you can and achieving a true balance - you are a superwoman!

The qualities of a superwoman have also given me the courage to become the woman whom despite the life changes she is experiencing, she chooses wisely, practices self-care and respects herself enough to rest, willing to make compromises, enjoy moments in time and take action where she can. By not giving up on what I believe, I felt that becoming a superwoman is a journey where if I wasn't prepared to grow into the transition from being a single woman to becoming a wife, a mother, then there were possibilities that I could fail in my home. I think some traits in no particular order have helped me along the way of discovering and making some life-changing decisions to become a superwoman who can achieve a balance on her personal life and work life. I also believe that inside every woman, there is a superwoman who by her own definitions and terms, is still able to maintain healthy wellbeing. As I share with you the qualities of my ideal superwoman, I would like you to think about what your ideal superwoman is?

In her home

It surely takes some time to process your new life as a wife or mother. It took me some time to decide whether or not I wanted to take an early maternity leave and whether I wanted to return to work at all after birth. Taking some time out for yourself and family, helps you to be more assertive and also makes you understand the needs of your family. A superwoman:

- Makes the home feel like a safe place

- Gets out of bed before anyone else

- Is observant about the needs of her family

- Is always willing to make compromises

- Manages the finances of her home with her husband

- Has the spirit of perseverance

1. **In her career**

Never give up on yourself. You have to put yourself out there. You can still build a name for yourself professionally. It's important to continue working on things that challenge you and not become stagnant in your home. Prove to yourself and others that you can do more and be better, while committed to your responsibilities in your home. A superwoman:

- Is driven and passionate about life

- Is persistent and doesn't give up easily on her goals

- Is ambitious and able to multitask her working demands

- Is committed and dedicated to her passion

2. In her lifestyle

A woman grows to understand how to achieve a balance between her professional and personal life. Once in her matrimonial home, her lifestyle begins to change in some areas of her life, the things she used to do as a single woman is no longer a part of her and so she begins to seek wisdom from above to be able to strike a balance between her personal and professional life. A superwoman:

- Has a simplified and organised life

- Influences people with a positive attitude

- Financially savvy and manages the finances of the home

- Looks good and takes care of herself

- Pays attention to daily practices for spiritual, mental and emotional well-being

3. In her relationships

Even with all what was going on in my life, I started developing self-control, taking control of my habits and choices and started to phase out some friendships. A superwoman:

- Puts God first as the centre of her life

- Works on becoming spiritually, mentally and emotionally mature

- Builds a great relationship with her husband

- Chooses her friends wisely

- Is a role model for other women who are inspired by her growth

4. In her attitude

I started believing more in my strengths by becoming realistic in my expectations. Self-confidence became a developing trait with the ability to control my emotions and behave responsibly. It helped me remember that no matter the circumstance, I should remain courageous. A superwoman:

- Enhances her strengths and places less emphasis on her weakness

- Is not afraid of changes

- Has to be bold, courageous and in control of her emotions

- Is not afraid of making mistakes and learning from them

A general trait I have discovered to become that 'superwoman' is knowing how to prioritise and manage my time. The difficult part is knowing when to let go and focus on doing the best you can and delegate the rest. Sometimes, becoming that superwoman could make you feel that you are capable of doing everything all by yourself - the perfect and independent woman but to become a superwoman, you must also realise that you can't achieve everything by yourself. Start by asking for help now and then (most especially at home) and don't be afraid to delegate to others. There were times I found it difficult to delegate tasks to others because I felt that no one else would be able to execute it better than I could or in the way I would expect. A superwoman can be confident, but shouldn't be over-controlling in trying to control every aspect of a situation or relationship. On the journey of becoming a wife and a mother, I learnt that wisdom is important. At times, my spouse and I would have different values on certain matters. We had different ways of approaching situations in our relationship. By talking about things properly and trying to understand each other's point of view, we were gradually able to establish the common ground but we are still learning to be better. I find that in some areas of our relationship if issues stay unresolved and swept under the carpet, it is most likely they'll come up again. I've also learnt that resolving our differences is not about trying to impose my beliefs because even if I may be right, being self-righteous doesn't help.

So depending on your perspective and personality, you can create your own list of what your "ideal superwoman" is. Keep in mind that to become that ideal superwoman you should have a vision for your life.

When I discovered I was pregnant while working a full-time job, it hit me at the moment that it meant that my career goals or ambition will suddenly take the back seat. I wondered what life would be like starting this whole new experience. Of course, the thought of motherhood was a bit scary at first, because it changes you but for the better and so I decided to accept this happening as a great blessing from God. The initial worry of what change this could bring and what it could mean for my career made me feel that my career aspirations and passion will also suffer due to lack of time. The good news about having a newborn is that your career ambition doesn't have to stop. You shouldn't feel that your life is going to take a drastic turn. Being a mom has helped me become more organised, more adaptable and also multi-task faster than I could before. Now, I've been able to embrace the good things and the good ways that I have changed, especially in my decision making. Sincerely, having a baby indeed changes your lifestyle in some ways, it becomes more hectic, lack of sleep, planning becomes complicated, might feel socially isolated after having a baby, but most importantly they make our lives better.

Becoming a parent could also put a strain on the marriage, because the amount of time you spend with your spouse going out, watching movies, or other hangouts significantly reduces once you have a baby. That time now goes to changing diapers, making bottles, or catching up on household chores. There's little time for you and your spouse to spend together, but you learn new ways to bond with your spouse as you care for your baby. How have I managed to find a balance with motherhood and marriage? By not being too hard on myself to be the perfect mother or perfect wife, but encouraging myself that no matter what I am going through - physically, emotionally and spiritually even through the tough days and the sleepless nights, I just know that I am the best mother in the world to my little one, and will continue finding the inner strength to maintain a positive mind and also embrace my emotions even in the darkest moments. It also comes with communicating more with my partner, on our concerns and just working together to figure things out as new parents.

If you are expecting a newborn or already have children, be encouraged and see this journey as a joyful experience to re-route your plans to find a new way of making things work for you, your children and your spouse. Now, I find myself spending a lot of time with my little boy, and when he's having his nap, that for me means "mummy's time" - an opportunity to work on family goals, work on my business, write my blogs, and amongst other things, do what needs attention at home. Although you may not get to finish everything you've planned to do in one day; but with every little time that you spend revisiting your inspiration/goals, it reignites your passion and brings you closer to fulfilling your heart desires.

Let's think of it this way, you will have children, they'll all grow up and settle down with their partners someday. You wouldn't want to look back at those years of parenting and wonder where time has gone or you wish you had done more when you had the chance. The key here is learning how to balance motherhood without losing your identity in the process. Having a work-life plan will help you determine whether you are heading in the right direction or not. I've always envisioned where I would like to see myself in the next 5 years in my career, but having to maintain a healthy work-life balance was one aspect of my life that was a necessity.

Conversation with Lawunmi Nwaiwu

Q. 1   How did you successfully practice a married life and work balance?

A. 1   It takes some sacrifices and re-prioritizing what's necessary to make time for my work, life and relationships. It may seem impossible especially when you're trying to juggle time with your family against all of your responsibilities but it's a gradual process, and with time, you will begin to find a healthy balance. I turned into an early riser to take care of home responsibilities and map out my tasks for the day to keep me from feeling overwhelmed.

Q. 2   You wrote about the worry of not reaching your milestones. What advice can you give to people who feel they have missed their milestones in life?

A. 2   We all have plans and goals for ourselves and as we get older we wonder if we'll ever achieve our dreams/goals but you shouldn't spend all your time comparing yourself to everyone else. Just because you are not doing the same thing as everyone, or haven't accomplished your personal goals at a certain age doesn't mean you have failed. So I learnt not to be too hard on myself and continue working towards my dream.

Q. 3   As you look back on some of the expectations you had before your marriage. How have they changed now?

A. 3   Having good and realistic expectations encouraged me to get married for the right reasons and now I understand better the challenges in a marriage, in areas of communication, commitment and patience. My values in these areas have now changed from living single life to being married.

Q. 4   What special role has your faith in God played in your marriage?

A. 4   My first year of marriage has taught me many things and has brought me closer to my faith because I've come to realise that a home cannot be successful on its own. As a woman, it comes with a lot of perseverance and believing that you are not alone as long as you keep holding on to your faith especially in the challenging times.

To be or not to be married!

It's common to hear the word 'marriage' and get nervous by the thoughts of the life commitments and changes that come with it. I remember getting married was pushed to the bottom of my goals in life, most especially in my early 20s because I was ambitious and at that point in my life "married" to my career. Many of us feel that the right time to get married is after we are financially stable, have a set of qualifications, own a home, or have hit certain milestones in our lives.

Getting married is a lifestyle choice. I remember while I was dating/in a relationship, as much as things were going smoothly, it wasn't enough reason for me to rush to the altar, getting married requires more than just love. Personally, it is more of having someone who shares the same values, wants the same things in a relationship as I do and both minds mutually agreeing on how to sustain the relationship through love and commitment. I didn't want to get married because it's a requirement to be met. Pursuing any relationship with marriage in mind could only lead to wrong intentions and so by letting my relationship evolve naturally into thoughts of marriage is key.

It's possible that in some cultures around the world, the parents may put pressure on you to settle down, some to extend the family lines. Sometimes there's no brushing them completely off this topic but what I always kept telling myself was that "a wedding may be for a day but marriage is for a lifetime - if I chose right".

I used to be scared of the thoughts of spending the rest of my life with someone because it meant starting new innings of your life but as I got older, I started learning to develop realistic expectations, gaining more knowledge to guide me towards choosing a partner wisely and preparing for a lasting union. So what were the signs that I was ready for a lifetime commitment?

It takes time to truly get to know someone and it also comes with having to make a decision either to get what we want or we learn to be happy with what we have.

It got to that point in my life where I was prepared to make an ongoing effort in the relationship because it gradually felt like I was with someone who was on the same page as me, and so the next mature and responsible thing to do was to do whatever it takes to maintain the relationship for a lifetime. When you are both on the same page on values and goals, continuous hard work and communication can help in overcoming any obstacle in the relationship.

Most people, especially the single ones find themselves making wrong decisions once they feel that time is against them. Getting married for the wrong reasons is just as bad as getting married to the wrong person - either getting married because of circumstances or any other hidden agenda. Most of my friends were already married by their mid-20s; I got married by 30 and I am glad it happened when the time was right. How would you know when the time is right?

You would have a clear reason why you want to get married. You have both understood each other to the point that you are able to resolve conflicts together. When you both start planning your future together, making long term goals and seeing the commitment in the relationship - these are signs that you are both ready to plan a marriage together, not a wedding.

No more excuses

Dropping the excuses

3 ways to put action on your dreams

Conversation with Lawunmi Nwaiwu

Something to think about

No More Excuses

"People often say that motivation doesn't last. Well, neither does bathing - that's why we recommend it daily".

- **Zig Ziglar**

It's always the year resolutions, the new year goals. When it comes to New Year's Eve, many see it as a time for a fresh start, but the majority of people still fail to see them through and forget about it few weeks into the start of the new year. If you find yourself setting yearly goals for yourself but never achieve any of them, start with a few questions. Are you setting realistic expectations for yourself? Do your goals involve a lot of thinking and not enough doing? Many of us seek inspiration and knowledge, which is all well and good; but if we do not apply them into our lives and fail to take action, it stops us from moving forward to success and it means you need a new approach.

Before writing down my yearly goals, I needed to ask myself what I needed to improve on and why it was so important to me. Growing up in Nigeria, I always had an entrepreneurial streak since childhood. The family I grew up with owned a bakery and I was inspired by the entrepreneurial mindset of establishing and managing a lucrative business. It was then I started becoming attracted to the idea of starting my own small business in future. Reflecting on my early years, entrepreneurship sparked my interest in creative thinking - looking at problems or situations from a fresh perspective, always wanting to excel in school projects or competitively involved in sports activities. I didn't know what the vision was then but one thing I knew was that I was very organised. I always saw a better approach to putting things in order, paying attention to every little detail to ensure perfection. I gradually discovered that I had a mindset of solving problem and was quite inquisitive about things in general. I remember whenever anything was broken, whether it was any furniture or assembling a new product, I was so eager to fix! My family would say I was always so particular about things, enjoyed putting things in a well-organised structure. During my youth, my clothes were always so stacked up and colour coded neatly in my wardrobe, my dressing table was arranged and I would pay attention to each item, grouping them accordingly to what they are i.e.

perfumes together, hair sprays together. Well, some may call it OCD (obsessive-compulsive disorder), but I'd rather call it an organisation skill. These are the very little traits that probably prepared me for the real world. Being organised is a skill that was transferrable into other areas of my life today; planning weddings, organising corporate events and also being organised in my home.

The key point here is that sometimes we ignore the very little skills we have and find them very insignificant without knowing that they will prove useful one day. I believe my entrepreneurial approach started from a young age and even if I wasn't able to employ staff then, I taught myself skills on how to be more creative, independent and resourceful. Participating in small social gatherings and demonstrating leadership and teamwork in some areas in church broadened my experience. I acquired more knowledge and skills through self-learning a couple of years after starting my business.

As time went on, I explored other interests i.e. how to design and manage a website, create new web contents, market my business, so I wouldn't have to rely or wait on people to get things done for me as a start-up. When I officially launched my wedding planning company in 2013, I was responsible for creating marketing strategies to create awareness for my business. I did it all, you name it - door to door leaflets and business card distribution, writing blogs, creating content for my social media platforms and website, attending networking events, event seminars and many more.

Setting smaller goals

Some of us have some memories from our childhood that may have inspired us to achieve some of the things we have today. We all have a story to tell and we all have people in our lives that may have positively influenced us. I learnt some lessons in the early years of starting my business. It has transformed my approach to making strategic decisions in the business. Nobody can be more passionate and driven about your business than you. Through self-learning on how to write blogs and manage a website, this developed into a personal skill for me which also led to having a passion for writing. That was how I released my first book - *starting a wedding planning career with limited funds*.

It is within our power to make big things happen. Some of us make excuses for not reaching our goal. Before you make the next excuse, stop and ask yourself - what can you do to be better? What can you change about your habits, values, thoughts or perception of life to be able to accomplish your goals? Make an honest decision and start with little steps. Don't pursue goals that do not make sense to you. Chasing goals that align with your values and priorities is what brings happiness.

I started setting small goals, to begin with, simply because small goals are easier to achieve. It creates that flexibility to adapt to new information or changes. There were also wild and big goals that even I felt was going to be more of a challenge to achieve but I made a commitment to myself that no matter the setbacks in the process, I will keep going, in the belief that the challenges of today will become tomorrow's victory.

There are moments in life that we need that big challenge to push us to reach our greatest potential, else we'll never get to know our full potential. How do you do that? By staying persistent. There are some goals, you cannot achieve on your own. Sometimes, to move forward, you need the help of others to push you, to help push past your limits, to help remain motivated, and take more action to reach where you want to go. The starting point may be scary, it's possible to feel the fear of doing something new and out of your comfort zone; but if we are not ready to make mistakes and learn from it, we will never get to live to our true potential.

Keep trying until you get it right

It is paramount to have a vision and long term goal but always make sure you break this down into smaller achievable goals so that you can stay motivated and determined to succeed. My first business client was a school friend. Although we never really communicated in school, we connected and kept in touch on Facebook. She knew about my company through my blogs and social media promotions. Her wedding request became my first official breakthrough in the wedding industry. She believed in me and my professional services and entrusted me to deliver an exceptional event. Her big day was fast approaching and I remember nervously going through my notes the night before the wedding, making sure that every detail of the wedding was covered. I needed to demonstrate my practical experience and so every detailed aspect of the wedding was crucial. I had packed everything I would need the night before and what kept racing through my mind were these three little words - I got this! On the morning of the wedding, it somehow felt like I was the one getting married - I was overly excited and anxious about the flow of the day and in that moment I prayed that everything would go well. At the wedding reception, the bride looked very beautiful in her wedding dress, although nervous but happy at the same time. We were finally celebrating her big day and it was my duty to make sure the day ran as smoothly as possible.

Many times, we find ourselves second-guessing ourselves when it comes to decision-making or when it comes to facing our fears. Many of us panic and curl back into our comfort zone. Whenever you encounter a challenge or obstacle or tell yourself that you are too caught up with the busy lifestyle, inexperienced, or you don't have the necessary resources to kick-start your future - you are only hindering your growth. I stopped being afraid of my weaknesses and started fighting to overcome the limitations through acceptance. It doesn't matter what obstacle you may presently be facing. If you see beyond the situation and believe that you have the inner power to overcome it, your fears will be eliminated. It is said that failure is unavoidable. It is inevitable that at some point during your life, you will fail but be prepared to get back on your feet and try again until you get it right. I've failed a couple of times in the past. One or two failed ideas knocked down my confidence for a short time and that's when I came to realise the importance of having the right people around you. They remind you that you are not a failure. Failing today does not make you a failure. It's more of a preparation for you to succeed. Since then, it's been an impactful journey to always have the 'never-give-up' attitude.

You don't need anyone to validate you

Before releasing my first book, there were times while writing it that I'd feel it was probably a bad idea launching a book. There were doubts and fear that no one would be interested in buying my book. I wondered how my book would stand out from the crowd, as a self-publisher. So there were a lot of questions on how my book would stand out? Is my book original enough? I was afraid that my book might make me look stupid. I was scared that it might upset people. However, I focused on starting with what I know, writing personal stories, reminding myself of why I started writing in the first place. Writing helped me to understand a lot more about myself by helping me make sense of my experiences and that is why it was important for me to share my life experiences with others who might be going through similar situations and hopefully get inspired. If it was only one person I could inspire with my story, then it's all good. It's a starting point to reaching out to others if I continue writing good contents. I've achieved a few milestones in my life and I am happy even with the little that has been accomplished because I know that it will gradually lead to bigger results. If you are thinking of writing a book, it's easier to think that your book might be invalid, but a book can be valuable if the knowledge within it is usable to the readers. If it's useful, it will sell.

I don't want to fail

Whenever you think of trying something new or taking some risks, remember that there is always a chance that you could fail. If you keep making excuses to avoid the risk of failing, then you are never going to try anything new. There were times things didn't go exactly as planned, especially during my early years of wedding planning. I remember the days that I'd get home, wishing that I could turn back the hands of time and make things right; but I can't. So we move forward and the only way forward was to learn from my mistakes and get rid of the self-pity. Planning a couples' wedding can be hectic and challenging. It takes a lot of patience and perseverance; using the right approach to be able to deliver good customer service to couples, ensuring that it is the happiest day of their lives, staying within budget and sticking to a schedule. It is a rewarding career and I saw it as an opportunity to demonstrate my organisation skills, my professionalism in coping with the stress and pressure that comes with it because it takes grace to be able to handle difficult clients.

When you have a passion for a career that truly excites and invigorates you, you'll find fresh ways of keeping that passion alive despite any challenging period in your life. Developing a passion to succeed will raise your game, it will change your way of thinking and drive you to achieve your desired results. Making excuses because you are scared to make a mistake will only draw you away from the best learning experiences that could have been valuable to you. You may feel that you may be judged for making a mistake. Instead, try and consider the ways that they may actually add strength to your character. The mistakes I've made in the past have brought out the best in my personal development. My failings have unleashed new skills that have been beneficial in my life; mistakes that even when I look back to the past, all I can see is how they have shaped my body of knowledge.

Conversation with Lawunmi Nwaiwu

Q. 1   In your life, you have experienced the highs and lows. Do you think a person needs to first overcome serious setbacks or challenges to be truly successful?

A. 1   Many of my life lessons learnt were through mistakes and failures, and that prepared and made me stronger. I've experienced challenges in some areas in my life where I was rejected for potential jobs, fear of what others may think etc. So you just need to learn how to adapt and not be afraid to keep challenging yourself because that's how you learn and grow.

Q. 2   In what way is it important to know your limitations in your life or career?

A. 2   One of the things I always remind myself is that success is not built alone. You can't do everything by yourself. At times you need others to help achieve your dream. Approaching someone that knows better than you does not make you look weak, and that is why during my career, I learnt to ask for help where necessary. Knowing our limits helps us to organise investments of our time, energy and other resources.

Q. 3   If you had the power to solve one and only one problem in the world, what would it be and why?

A. 3   I've always believed that education is power but the barrier to work opportunities is becoming more of a bigger issue or challenge for the youths and graduates. So making a positive impact on career jobs is probably where my effort would be most effective.

~ Something to think about ~

1. What is your talent? Think about what you are good at. Ask a couple of your friends/family what they would identify as your biggest assets.

2. What inspires you? Where do you find inspiration to move forward - books, websites, family, leaders?

3. How do you respond to what others say about you? One can choose to react negatively or choose to ignore it. Remember your actions and words define you.

4. How can you make yourself better? You can either give up and accept your circumstances or choose to find ways to improve on yourself.

5. What do you think your purpose is? This is a deep question but with time, you will gradually begin to discover your purpose in life.

My Author-Preneur Journey

Growing up, my dream was to own a business, although I wasn't sure what line of business but I've always had that entrepreneurial mindset because I was surrounded by family and friends who owned businesses. It encouraged me to live a more organised life and feel the constant need to improve my skills and take continuous action on small ideas until I was able to figure out my true passion.

After completing my master's degree at London Metropolitan University, I longed for something bigger and knew I needed a change.

I wanted to step outside of my comfort zone, free myself from distractions and challenge myself to grow and explore my career interests.

I decided to take a one-year internship in hospitality and events in Orlando, Florida. My mother was very surprised and confused about my intentions to intern in a new environment, to experience a different working culture, and also being away from home but something deep down kept attracting me to the idea of exploring my career interests in Orlando. Needless to say, that decision was one of the best decisions of my life because it was a great opportunity to get my feet wet and experience the real world of business. During my internship, I was able to gain international experience along with the knowledge and skills I learnt on the job. I had the chance to network with professionals working in that part of the world.

After completing my internship, I came back to the UK and even though I was keen on getting a job that matched my credentials, I was unlucky. Instead, I got miniature jobs of basic salary but that didn't discourage me. I was still driven to start my own business, to do what I truly enjoy and with the right mindset, I started talking to people that were not in my "comfort zone". I started doing some little things to increase my self-confidence and experience in events. I got better by learning from my mistakes, getting involved in organising church events, youth conferences and event shows. Occasionally, I'd help a couple of friends in coordinating their private functions and that was how my journey to becoming a wedding planner started.

A Business Without any Client

My journey also had its highs and lows because I needed to learn perseverance, most especially when people doubted my abilities. I didn't get my first client till after a year I started out on my own. It was a challenging phase of my life because while I was working a 9 to 5 office job and I also needed to be consistent with my side business. It seemed almost impossible, but I wasn't ready to quit.

So, to increase my knowledge about my services, I decided to put more time into writing blogs, networking and reading wedding-related contents, and figuring out the hangout spots of potential clients. I didn't take a wedding planning course but by attending entrepreneurial events, conferences, wedding exhibitions, seminars, volunteering in some events and looking for leadership opportunities around me, it gave me more self-confidence to lead a team of wedding vendors and develop my entrepreneurial skills. I started venturing into bigger projects by starting a fundraising event and wedding fairs, which allowed me to practice my time management, organisation, leadership and teamwork skills. I have learnt from my mistakes in the planning process of these projects and it has not in the least bit discouraged me from my passion; in fact, it pushed me to never give up on myself. At this point, I had a very clear focus and direction of my career, with a determination to overcome the challenges of business growth.

Since I started my journey, I have certainly had some interesting learnings along the way, which has helped me become better personally and also professionally. So I decided to share my experience with other aspiring young entrepreneurs who are yet to experience their career path or inspire those in similar situations that need the encouragement to rediscover their true passion by writing about my journey. I have also experienced self-discovery through writing, it helps me connect with myself, understand my life and my thoughts, self-reflect on life's memories and clear the clutter from my mind. It's not actually easy writing a book or putting some aspects of your life out there to the world and even though I was nervous about releasing my first book *"Starting a Wedding Planning Career with Limited Funds [2015]"* and then my second book *"Secrets to a Work-Business Balance [2017]"*; I noticed the more I become aware of my progress, the more involved I feel in making it continue to grow. My writing journey was inspired by a book author coach, Tunji Olujimi [CEO of Accelerated Authors Academy] who not only encouraged me to write my first book but also coached me on how to self-publish my first book. He encouraged and helped jumpstart my writing career.

How do I keep igniting my passion?

Watching some TV shows have truly contributed and positively impacted my journey as an entrepreneur. To name a few, The Apprentice UK and Dragon's Den have really inspired me and driven my passion and business acumen. I remember I started watching these shows after relocating to the UK and they became my favourites. One of the major things The Apprentice show taught me is that it's all about teamwork, not 'I'. It's a competitive show which consists of about 11-15 candidates with professional backgrounds to compete for Alan Sugar's six-figure salary to become his business partner. The show also broadened my knowledge of real-life business situations and how to think creatively on your feet. The on-screen tasks revealed a lot of truth about the real world of business. It taught me that communication, showing reliability and leadership skills is what makes a good business person.

Many times, I'd wish I could be on the show, competing with other candidates and demonstrating my business acumen. I always wondered what position I'd be now if any of these business leaders had invested in my business; of course, it would have been a huge dream come true for me. Sometimes, watching TV shows that are in line with your interests really helps in determining whether it is something you'll like to build a career on. TV shows like Dragon's Den are about real business and investment. Then, I would never miss an episode of this TV show because it welcomed various entrepreneurs who would pitch their business ideas to a panel of venture capitalists in the hope of securing investment from them. Theo Paphitis and Duncan Bannatyne were my favourite dragons, in fact, I used to visit a few of Duncan's Spas to relax with friends.

You may not get to enter some of these shows but you can gain educational knowledge of how business works, how to identify business risks and opportunities, how to demonstrate leadership and how to understand more about your market by watching the TV shows. There are free resources out there that we can make use of, for our self-development.

As you decide on your entrepreneurial journey, remember to surround yourself with good people, those who can inspire you so good things can happen. I hope this story will inspire and motivate others to take their entrepreneurial leap, a journey to achieving greatness.

Your Story Matters, you Matter

Starting your own journey

Discovering your true identity

Conversation with Lawunmi Nwaiwu

Something to think about

Become your own story

"An ordinary life lived exceptionally well".

- **Jan Fortune**

Most of us struggle to be ourselves and not somebody else or we try to please everybody but ourselves. Some of us want to start a business but are more concerned with how others might perceive us, worried about saying the wrong things or not fitting in with the crowd. Overthinking these things will only lead to you not doing anything at all and thinking you're being judged even when that's not the case. You need to give yourself credit. Others may have started making their millions before you but that doesn't mean you can't. You only hinder your growth if you continue thinking you have nothing to offer and that you can't make an impact on someone's life. Just being you is the starting point because nobody else is living your life. People might have their opinions or ideas but the only person who knows what is best for you is you. Be your own boss if you have to. Others may not like it, but so what! Others may not like your way of thinking or doing things but if you keep believing in yourself, getting your desired results, others will have no choice but to believe in you.

What inspires you?

I gave up wanting to please everybody because I realized I will only drive myself insane trying to do so. You can take a look at what other people are doing to see what inspires and encourages you about them. We can learn powerful lessons from those who inspire us. It could be our boss, a public figure, partner, or friend who has accomplished great things. I get inspired by people who know where they are going and strive to accomplish their goals and do so enthusiastically with hope. I enjoy their company because it energises me. It refreshes my mind with much confidence that I am capable of achieving greater things if I am determined to accomplish my goals. I am also inspired by leaders who share their inspirational stories that I can relate to. It helps me refocus on my own strength, work on my weaknesses and implement change.

I remember when I used to watch The Oprah Winfrey show. I would watch her show thinking to myself that I want to be like her; I want to share my story and inspire others! She was doing that across the globe, connecting with international audiences on her talk show, highlighting global issues on poverty and child abuses. She became an inspiration to me because she embodies the ambitious and self-driven woman that I aspire to become. In those moments, I'd feel worried that because I am not an extrovert, I may not be able to meet new people and engage freely.

However, while having a reflection on myself, I came to accept that I wasn't going to be that extreme extrovert. Yes, I can be outgoing and socially confident to some extent but it usually takes a while for me to engage in interactions freely with others. I'd consider myself more of an introvert who enjoys time alone and could get emotionally drained after spending a lot of time with others. Honestly, if this also sounds like you, there is nothing wrong with that. If it is not a "bad introvert" then it is not a personality issue to worry about. If you are like me, it just means you are quite reserved, you are a thoughtful individual and an active listener with a loving and caring at heart. Don't look to others to define who you are or what your purpose should be. It's okay to be you. Avoid comparing yourself to others.

I'm discovering more about myself, as I live my daily life. I enjoy writing and sharing my experiences in a simplified and honest way that people can relate to. As a wedding planner, competing amongst other professional wedding planners didn't kill my vision because I was driven and determined to grow my business, figure out my USP and let my personality reflect through my work. Brand personality is an important part of growing your business because it helps customers feel more connected and comfortable buying into your brand. So, focus on being your authentic self and not someone else, because it's when you're genuine that you'd attract the right people to yourself.

When I started writing my first book, I was scared that nobody would connect or relate to my content. After the book launch, I was pleased to see people connecting with me through my blog and were also writing short and inspirational contents on my life experiences.

To truly express yourself better, you need to discover yourself first

Find power in your identity

Rule 1 - Stop pleasing others but yourself.

It can only lead to a loss of your identity - if you keep hiding the unique things about yourself which makes you the amazing individual that you already are; you will lose your true self. I lost a few friends along the way, some felt my lifestyle wasn't socially wild enough, which was okay because I wasn't about to wreck my self-esteem and make myself uncomfortable just to please them. Gradually, I started learning to be comfortable with the fact that there will be some people who might disapprove of me no matter what I do. Having confidence in the daily decisions will show others that you truly know what you are doing.

Rule 2 - Stop doubting yourself.

When I started dating, at first I had interesting points of what I wanted my ideal life partner to be. I had this whole mentality of wanting to pay for my meal; whether or not the guy offered to pay. When going on dates, we can anticipate the conversations, the hangout experience, what you may think of each other, how interested you might be etc. It's possible that you find out that you both seem to have values that conflict but it doesn't necessarily mean you need to abandon those values. Instead, consider it as what makes you different especially if they are values that make you feel more true to yourself. For example, if someone thought I was acting in too serious because I turn down invitations to some social places that I know I wouldn't fit in or places that would make me uncomfortable, that's me taking control of my life. It's about taking bold decisions on some life choices that will make me feel good about myself without feeling coerced into doing the opposite.

Over the past years, I went on the journey of discovering my true self and dedicating time to get to know myself. I started being honest and open about certain aspects of my life. I started asking myself some really hard questions. Questions like: Why don't I do more of the things I love? If money wasn't an issue, is there anything I would want to do?

To learn more about yourself, you need to ask yourself more questions about who you are, and also you have to be honest with the answers. I started appreciating my individuality, embracing my flaws and putting things into perspective since my mid-20s. However, it is never too late to re-discover yourself even after a certain age. We are all imperfect and at times, the imperfect side of you is what others may love more about you. It is a difficult journey being yourself in a world that almost every day of your life feels like it wants to change you. We struggle with lifestyle, faith, identity, community and culture, to be able to find ourselves and know who we are. It happens sometimes that when I am in a room full of strangers, either at work or a social event, it'd get so overwhelming for a minute because different personalities in that small room have different perspectives on life. Few who are very socially engaged, others who are professionals, I'd never really know how to interact. At times I could feel myself doing more of the listening than talking, few nods every now and then to show I'm pretty much switched on in between conversations and analyse every movement or words repeatedly in my head before engaging. Some moments can be quite intense, especially if it was a one-on-one discussion and just from the first few secs I could already predict how the conservation was going to flow, or what I'd need to say to avoid the awkward silence. This was a concern for me and I started to feel maybe I was anti-social, not funny or I just have the 'I-don't-know-what-to-say' syndrome.

Several reasons came to mind. It could be that I was not prepared to get out of my regular world of interests, worried about saying something stupid or feeling the need to say something right. So, I made a decision to flip things around. I was determined not to be defined by this. What had helped me overcome this was to:

- Establish a good rapport

- Not overthink

- Observe and take in my surroundings and relax

- Be more open and enthusiastic

- Share my experience or interests

I focused on bringing out the beauty in me by identifying my strengths, hobbies, achievements, aspirations and beliefs. If others are happy to talk about things that excite them, so can you, even if you don't exactly share the same interests. Gradually, I no longer felt intimidated or unable to voice my own opinion without having to act, to talk, or look in a certain way to fit in.

I no longer felt I needed to act, talk, or look in a certain way to be in someone's life. I worked on my self-confidence and started trusting myself that I am enough to be loved for who I am.

Tell your story

Sharing your story helps you make sense of your life, reflecting on the past and the present. It helps to make sense of why certain events in your past happened the way they did. It helps you gain a fresh and better perspective on the way you see life, situations, people, from many different views.

Sometimes, we are so stuck in the situation of our own lives that it takes another person to give us a fresh perspective on what's going on or how to go about things.

I realised that a lot has changed in my life since I stopped dwelling on things that I can't change or on the things of the past. Instead, I started focusing on the things that I can actually control - we may not be able to control the storm that's coming but we can control our effort and attitude towards it by preparing for it. I also focused on changing my behaviour, identifying my worries and working on them. I started thinking of what I would do if my business was to fail rather than having the mindset that I don't want my business to fail. Sometimes when we assume the worst scenario that could happen, we will be able to put more energy into ensuring that our fears do not hinder us from growing.

I find that life has become easier to manage since I started writing, sharing my experience with others. It has helped me reflect on so many areas in my life. I don't write because I want to solve other people's problems but I enjoy helping readers find the place within themselves where they can discover and uncover the inspiration they need to move towards a particular solution needed in their lives. My blogs simply reflect on my own need to allow wisdom greater than mine to flow in a way that I can learn and grow. So that when people read, it may resonate with something going on in their own lives and possibly get in touch and share their own perspective from their various experiences. Today, many millennials and young adults seem to get frustrated when they see that things are not going as hoped or feel stuck in a situation that seems like the end of the road - feeling like they will never reach the desired destination of success. When we share our own story on life lessons learnt, how we were able to embrace our own journey to overcome our storm, we step out of our comfort zone, giving us a clear direction of where we are going and in the process, we are able to awaken future generations to their potential too.

There is power in telling your story. I am no longer ashamed of what has happened in the past because I find so much peace within because I choose to let go of the past or circumstances that have made me feel like I don't matter. Our story is what makes us able to connect with others out there who aren't ready just yet. I have had someone ask me why I share my vulnerability with the world - what I've been through, in my blogs or previous books? And I thought to myself, I'm okay with sharing some chapters of my life, which is not for everyone. It's for readers who may need that story they can relate to, that inspiration that might encourage them to never give up on themselves.

Don't let anyone make you feel ashamed of your past or shortcomings. Some people might have written you off, called you names, and expected nothing of you but there is always light at the end of the tunnel.

Conversation with Lawunmi Nwaiwu

Q. 1   Why was it important for you to share your own story?

A. 1   I share my story because it is these past experiences that have shaped me. There have been ups and downs and I hope sharing it with others who are yet to experience such may one day inspire them. I share my story so that it can bring strength to a lot of people and motivate them to keep pressing on. I am stronger today because of everything I went through and sharing my journey with the world has also given me an added reassurance that my past no longer has control over me.

Q. 2   Which do you think you have most: talent, intelligence, education, or persistence? How has it helped you in your life?

A. 2   Oh wow. I'll probably go for talent and persistence. What I discovered about myself is that I am very driven and passionate about whatever I set my heart to do. I hate the excuses of "I don't think it will work" syndrome without even trying or that "there are limited resources". I like to know that I have given all my best before giving up, having the determination to succeed has always been my driving force. I also enjoy trying new things to discover what more potential I may have.

~ Something to think about ~

Some steps have helped me discover my true self, which might be useful to you in bringing out the super confident and beautiful *you*.

1. **Find your own voice** - The power of social media can have either a positive or negative influence in our lives. Living a life constantly feeding on the opinion of others, relying on and seeking for likes and comments on these platforms could only fuel negative thoughts in the mind; just because you feel you need the validation of others to feel accepted. Start by putting away all the social media distractions that make you feel reassured by the likes and comments of others and get to know yourself more, on a higher level. You can start by setting goals for yourself, reading inspirational books, or paying attention to other things that will help you find confidence in your own voice without listening to other people's opinions.

2. **You can't please everybody** - Not everyone will like or accept you. Others will love you because they love what you do or can relate to you on common interests. Everyone will not buy into your brand if you start a business; but if you believe in your vision and you are making progress, others will begin to believe and be attracted to your brand. Your relationship with close friends or work colleagues doesn't mean, you are not responsible for making them feel comfortable in every way, and in the process neglecting your own feelings. You are responsible for your own happiness and it starts by not preventing yourself from living your best life.

3. **Appreciate who you are** - I always appreciate the morals I was instilled with from my childhood. It has given me a clearer perspective on life by not letting others define me. By knowing who you are, what you stand for and what you need to do means you are not looking for permission from others to do what you already know you ought to do. Appreciate what you have and do not compare yourself to others. Everyone's destiny is different and that is why keeping a clear focus on your own journey will lead you to live the life you've always wanted and then you can share your experience with others.

4. **Be honest about the things you say and do** - Do you find yourself saying things just to please people even if you don't actually mean them? Do you find yourself acting a certain way around your boss only when he or she is around? Or find yourself living the lifestyle of your friends, even if doing so is hurting you deep down? We would only be damaging our true self just because we are afraid to be honest with our opinions so we don't upset anyone. The bottom line here is from the moment you start going against your values/beliefs, you are gradually damaging the special gifts that you have. There is nothing wrong in politely speaking the truth and respecting your friends' or colleagues' different ways of dealing with situations.

5. **It's all about you** - As selfish as this may sound, you need to start putting yourself first because you are responsible for your life. Only you can drive your own goals and dreams and get to where you've hoped to be. Start by changing your mindset and challenging yourself to push past all the excuses, fears and obstacles that have hindered you from being a step closer to success.

From the moment you begin to understand more about your personality, what you love and don't, where you come from and where you want to be; the more you will be able to gauge who you want to be and ultimately become the best version of yourself.

Finally, how do you find your voice? Think of something powerful you can say to yourself or something positive you desire to say to yourself. Keep repeating it out loud to yourself with confidence until you believe it.

The Emotional Detox

New beginnings and starting fresh

How to Let Go of your Emotional Baggage

Conversation with Lawunmi Nwaiwu

Something to think about

Begin the Emotional Detox

"We cannot solve our problems with the same thinking we used

when we created them".

- **Albert Einstein**

Have you ever felt like you are doing too much but it doesn't seem like you are doing enough? What do you do when you feel you are not accomplishing enough? Sometimes, do you feel you are trying to move forward but you see yourself going round in circles and wondering when things are ever going to turn around for you? Well, you are not alone because we've all been there.

You log in to your social media account and see feeds that your old friend from school is getting married. A couple in your neighbourhood just bought a house. Another friend has just given birth to triplets. You spot a family living lavishly. A former colleague who was on the same level as you has now been promoted to a higher level. You wish to have all of these things too but it just seems like progress is going super slow in your life.

I want you to start reading this chapter with these three words in your mind - 'YES, YOU CAN'! You can have it all but it means going through the process of transforming your life by making significant lasting changes. It starts from within, having that burning desire to have a better life by getting rid of all the emotional baggage that has held you back from progressing in life. Transforming your life emotionally involves going beyond the way you think and changing the way you live. You do this by using your thoughts, words, faith and action.

Whenever I am going through a season of transition in my life, I go to who I believe in, for his guidance, wisdom and direction on the necessary changes. It could be changes in my relationships, my family, my health, my home, my spiritual life, or my finances. Whichever one of these that has been a burden, I encourage you that this is the time to begin the transition journey.

Revisit your past

If you have experienced a traumatic event in your past, flashbacks into your past may sometimes cause your energy level to drop. Your anxiety level increases and your emotions are easily triggered. You need to work on this area of your life so you can experience emotional healing.

You might be aware of some of the changes that are going on and there are some that you wouldn't know. Most of the time, you may have received signs in your daily life that you don't really understand. Sometimes, you may have received a revelation through a message intended just for you and you already know the action you are to take - if you have, then that's great. If you haven't, don't worry, you can still receive your personal revelation. How I have received personal revelation is by getting closer to God. In my own little way and with prayers to support, I have faith about facing my fears, concerns and weaknesses. However, we all have different ways of receiving personal revelations. Some people may receive their revelation through motivational speakers, conferences, messages and more.

The key point here is that if we want to experience change, it begins with a new mindset, exploring new strategies to move us closer to our goals and living a life that pleases God. One of the hardest things in life is making the decision to press the reboot button. Do you ever feel you are asking God for something, but he's gone silent on you? You feel stuck and you start wondering if he's still there with you? During a situation in my life, day after day, I kept calling out to him. At a point, words could no longer come out of my mouth. I knew he was hearing me, I knew he was there with me, I knew he wanted me to just wait a little longer and be still. Yet, I'd find myself asking him what his plans for my life were, what direction he needed me to go, what exactly I needed to do next? All the tears, frustration, questions, arguments, dreams and desires I poured out to him and all I could hear him say was *"trust me"... "have you already forgotten who I am"...* and I'd respond saying, *"I haven't... but it's just so unclear right now and I am not seeing any changes... I have got pressing concerns, I feel it's only you I can talk to, open up and share everything with... others don't seem to get me like you do... and it's beginning to feel like I'm all alone in this right now... like for real where are you, Lord?"*

Change is not easy. I remember when I had to make a conscious decision to start attending church more regularly, be more committed and stop making reckless decisions. Not compromising my faith or beliefs to please anyone. Changes can be quite overwhelming. Leaving the old ways is a difficult transition but what about the "greater good" that awaits us if we let go of such baggage - letting go of the rage, disappointment, hatred and jealousy, to feel a new sense of purpose and direction; I think that's a great approach to living a healthy lifestyle. An example of the change I've experienced personally is dealing with unfairness. A long time ago, after losing a court case, I complained that things weren't fair.

Filled with anger, I was even more furious that God was watching me go through such injustice. I felt I wasn't treated fairly because someone who did wrong was favoured, and I wasn't for doing the right thing. In that moment, I cried out to God with my mom standing by me, she kept reassuring me with the words "Only God knows best". As much as I didn't really appreciate these words instantly, I gradually started to learn about God's ways in my life. We may go through trials and temptations, difficult times, but that does not mean that we should lose faith, even when things seem impossible. He just wants us to leave everything to him and trust in him. This was a painful and unfair memory which still lingers in my mind. I realised that it was not my case to win and grumbling about injustice wouldn't change anything. If I didn't lose that day, I probably wouldn't have rededicated my life to Christ. Having a deep conversation with God, sharing how I truly felt which reminded me of forgiveness. In doing so, I was able to move past the injustice and find myself again.

To let go of the emotional burden and the negative thoughts, I stopped letting people's problems weigh me down. I started getting my finances in order, I was more active in church, I started re-strategising my business growth and writing inspirational books. It's not all perfect yet, but I've started experiencing joy, contentment and peace with some of the choices I've made.

Here are a few detox tips that have helped me get through my emotional burdens. I hope it will guide you through the emotions that might have affected your growth mentally, spiritually and physically.

1. **Stress** - At times, we tend to worry a lot about the things that are going on in our lives. Most people take on too many responsibilities that later become a burden, especially if the situation spirals out of control, we start to feel stressed. Sometimes if our basic needs are not met, we tend to become anxious and under the pressure of finding a solution to the issue. What I've come to realise is that when I let stress or worry dominate my life, it means I have lost the ability to trust in God. Sometimes it is not easy to admit that we can't seem to manage our own life and because all the stress can wear us down; how to recover from it is important in our lives.

   Tips:

   a. *Recognise the problem*: Accepting that the lingering problem exists is the starting point to an honest self-evaluation and humble confession of yourself. Once you do, you will be able to have an ideal plan to relieve the stress and get the help needed. Don't be blinded by the fact that an area in your lifestyle needs more attention for things to get better and for you to get things done in an orderly manner.

   b. *Give yourself a break*: You can take a day to reflect on yourself. From time to time, I have a 'me' time, I involve myself in a hobby I enjoy doing. A break could give you a good and healthy lifestyle, so you feel energised and refreshed. To help reduce your workload, you should delegate your tasks when possible. I used to have a hard time letting others help due to the whole independent mentality because I feared that they might not understand or do things the way I wanted them done. Later, I came to realise that I was only burning myself out.

2. **Forgiveness** - Holding on to the past can affect the present. There have been moments in my life where I felt I was taken for granted especially in situations where I had put other people's problems first. I believe some people are put in our lives for a reason and a season. We are in a world where some will hurt you, disappoint you, even the ones you trust most are the ones who may take you for granted. People might take advantage of your generosity and kind

nature, even expect or demand more from you than they should. I stopped being hard on myself because it's a gift to be kind and being able to help others. To overcome the feeling of this burden, I started setting some boundaries and sticking to it. Forgiveness is difficult, especially when you feel hurt. When all you can feel is the urge of confronting those who have offended you or hurt them back the way they did to you. But I found solace in God, asking him to help me move on. There is this scripture (Romans 12:19) I've always turned to as a reminder of forgiveness - *"...If it is possible on your part, live at peace with everyone. Do not avenge yourselves, beloved, but leave room for God's wrath. For it is written: Vengeance is Mine; I will repay, says the Lord..."*

Tips:

a. *Forget the past*: Forgiveness is for our own growth and happiness. When we hold onto pain, resentment and anger it harms us far more than it harms the offender - this is why we have to let go. Be surrounded by a new environment of positivity, an environment that will not push you back to the memories of the past, be around people that will encourage you and bring out the happiness in you.

b. *It's time to heal*: Of course, forgetting the past is not an easy process but giving yourself a chance to heal is the starting process and it will then make you realise when the time is right for you to forgive, you would know it, and once you do, it will become a relief, a lifted burden and one of the greatest feelings you'll ever experience. You will no longer be giving someone else authority over your mind and heart.

3. **Give yourself a chance** - Many of us feel that we are not worth the big dreams or the good life we deserve. Give yourself a chance to grow. You may have missed out on big opportunities in the past, people may have mocked your current situation. The feeling that you have no chance to stand out because of the little education or zero expertise you have. Here's the good news! You can still be who you want to be as long as you are ready and determined to fight for what you want. Surround yourself with the right people who can

encourage you and support you on your journey. Many times in the past, I've been rejected from potential desired jobs. But I decided to give myself that opportunity to start up a small business that I was passionate about while still working a 9 to 5 job. Don't get discouraged if you couldn't start your career in your 20s. The right opportunity will still knock on your door at the right time. Give yourself a chance to be happy again, practice loving yourself rather than self-hate or self-pity. Accept your own flaws and take action by working on them. Whenever I felt life was tough, I would remember how tougher I am. I take life's setbacks as an opportunity to learn from the situation and grow. You mustn't give up on yourself, create goals and take action.

Tips:

a. *Quit comparing yourself to others*: Trying to live someone else's dream means you'd be forgetting your unique identity. Most people may give you advice on how they handled situations in their life and expect you to follow the same approach. Growing up, I was advised on certain areas in my life but I realised that no one can really tell you how to handle a situation in your life except you. Everyone's destiny is different. When a couple of my co-workers were getting achievement awards and I wasn't, I was happy for them but also started to wonder "They got an award - am I also going to get a promotion? What am I even doing in this company?". Little did I know that God was preparing me for greater achievement. Therefore, let's not get caught up in the fact that our friends are now on a different level, securing deals and opportunities, or because they found a job within a week when you have been unemployed for years. You are not them!

b. *Count your blessings*: Being alive is a greater blessing. Every day is an opportunity to have a fresh start. It is a new day, a new start. It doesn't matter what happened yesterday, all that counts is today. If you are in good health, you have a shelter, you have your loved ones around you and you have a job; be grateful. Start looking on the brighter side of life and keep having the faith that who you believe in, is bigger than all your problems. By nurturing your spirit, soul and body in faith, you are giving God a chance to carry out his plans in your life. We need to learn to appreciate what we have before time makes us appreciate what we had. I appreciate every single person in my life who has tried to brighten my days. It's the little things that matter the most.

c. *Give yourself the best chance of success*: Start focusing on what matters most. If we keep playing the safe option from making mistakes, we hinder our progress and hold ourselves back from achieving our full potential. When it comes to business and entrepreneurial endeavours, I've always believed in following my gut instincts and taking risks because if I don't, I may never know what the result could be. If we never come out of our comfort zone, we would never know or understand our self-worth. Taking a step to success may mean you might experience failure first but success is never perfect. I learnt a lot from writing my first book even though there was that fear that nobody would be interested but I kept pushing forward. It was one of the goals I was determined to achieve and I was ready to break down every barrier that was holding me back from my ambition.

Conversation with Lawunmi Nwaiwu

Q. 1 Why did you write about emotional detox, why is it an important chapter?

A. 1   My experience taught me that if I want my growth to be a long-lasting one, I need to let go of all the anger, hurt and resentment within my mind and body so that I can move towards a happier and healthier lifestyle. It's important for us to understand that if we want change, it starts with ourselves.

~ Something to think about ~

You need to be willing to find out who you are, what you can do and just how much potential you have to live the fullest life you can. Never stop learning how to grow and make yourself better. Begin the journey to focus on what matters most by setting long term goals and how you actually want to achieve them.

Be Thankful for Everything

The power of being thankful

Why you need a gratitude list

Conversation with Lawunmi Nwaiwu

Be Thankful for Everything

"When you are grateful, fear disappears and abundance appears".

-   Anthony Robbins

Being alive is the starting point of being thankful. I may not be living a lavish lifestyle but being alive in good health is the greatest gift that I cannot take for granted. As I reflect on my past, coming from an African origin and understanding the morals and values of our culture, there are childhood experiences that have been an important part of my personality; especially in the way I live, learn and behave. There's so much gratitude for not just what I have now but also for what I have had in the past. There are people in my past that I'm no longer in contact with but they have in one way or the other contributed to shaping me into who I have become today. My loved ones may have been strict in my upbringing but I can look back, with the acceptance that most of those teachings, scolding and advice have positively influenced my behaviour with greater happiness, having a greater sense of mission and purpose and higher levels of forgiveness. Most of us don't remember our first three years of life but our earliest experiences may stick with us and influence us well into adulthood.

There are some little things in life we take for granted. We get carried away by the things in other people's lives and think their lives is what we should be living. Being thankful for what you have and not try to take from others what isn't yours. By being thankful, you become healthier emotionally and physically. The more we appreciate every moment of the day, even when we're faced with challenges, the more strength we gain within.

For my upbringing, I am grateful to have had my loved ones around me. There were moments where I could have felt lonely not been around my mother but because of the love around me, I kept pushing forward. Don't get so carried away by wanting it all immediately or getting yourself too worried which is normal because you are human after all. You are allowed to get concerned over things that we do not have any control over but the key point is that whenever things get rough, we still need to be thankful. It is not easy to be thankful in every circumstance. I've come to learn that when we choose to thank God amid difficulty, it defeats the forces of darkness, it gives us the strength to trust and hope in faith that he will turn any situation around.

I am thankful for reconnecting with my dad in my late teens because it helped to block out all the negative emotions or hurt I may have felt growing up without a father figure. Reconnecting can be emotionally challenging but doing so with a good reason - for peace or healing of old wounds, can help us to take healthy steps in moving towards resolution. Focusing on our daily blessings, future opportunities can help us never to allow our challenges and struggles to interfere with our peace of mind. If we can take more time to think about all the things we ought to be thankful for, we will have little room for worry. By being thankful, we invite positivity and light into our lives and our homes. When we are thankful, it becomes contagious and it encourages others who may be going through tough times in their lives. It may be difficult to overlook the challenges we are experiencing and remain thankful but doing that is how we attract special blessings into our lives.

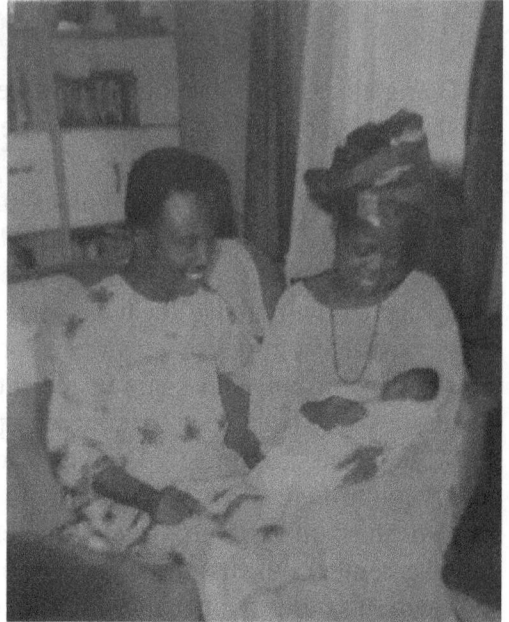

Many of us, when we start performing at a higher level, we start overlooking the very little things that make our life worth living. Some of us are guilty of only remembering to be thankful when we need something. I don't ever want to forget what God has done and is doing in my life. No matter how small or big, I don't want to take him for granted. He has done so much in my life since I rededicated my life to him and I have been experiencing changes. His grace has transformed me in every aspect of my life. Whenever I become impatient in my trying times, I often try to remind myself of how much he just wants the best for me and not forget to keep giving thanks to him even in the time of distress. Right now, you may be going through challenges that you don't even understand and find yourself questioning why such is happening to you. Sometimes you may not understand why you are going through your struggles but all you can do is to trust the right path you are on and maybe one day, you will understand why it all happened. Until that day, all we can do is to be grateful and be thankful for life.

Most of us have the privileges that others don't have and we forget to use it to inspire or change someone else's life. There are opportunities where we can use our privilege to speak or take action to address some issues and positively influence others - it could be at work, school or other communities. Today, I look back and I'm grateful for the relationships that didn't work out in the past, the ones that didn't progress to the next level and even some opportunities that probably weren't the right ones for me then. There's a reason for everything! A reason for the setbacks, the disappointments, the struggles and even the business opportunities we may have lost. If you also strongly believe in something like I do, you will begin to realise that everything in life does happen for a reason.

At this point, I would like you to pause for a moment to reflect and begin to feel appreciative for the millions of things going well in your daily life. What do you sometimes forget to be thankful for?

Let's be thankful for everything that happens in our lives; it's all an experience

---

Here are a couple of things I am grateful for and they also help me to be more appreciative and thankful:

1. **Being alive** - Being alive is a daily blessing and another chance to make things right. Some of us get so caught up with our everyday tasks, get ourselves stressed out and forget to live and enjoy the present moment. That is why life is the greatest blessing given to us. Tomorrow is never guaranteed that is why I work hard to achieve

the things that I am passionate about while I can and I also spend time with loved ones and enjoy everything we are blessed with.

2. **Good health** - Waking up every day in good health is something to be thankful for. Even if your health isn't great, it could be worse, also remember some other people might be in a critical condition, this is all the more reason why we need to be thankful for good health.

3. **Small circle of friends** - I've always kept a small circle of friends right from my childhood, even during my university days, at social places, or workplace and I've come to realise that it is not about the number of friends but the quality. There is no point having a large group of friends if none could help me make better lifestyle choices or contribute to my progress in one way or the other.

4. **My parents** - My parent's stern advice while growing up has helped me reach where I am today. Giving clear guidance and being there when I needed them is something I am very grateful to have experienced. Many a time we take them for granted but if we still have them in our lives, now is the time to build any bridge and create good long-lasting memories with them. My Mother has always been my role model. Her strength, her passion and discipline are traits that inspire me. I am also thankful for my father because, despite our distant relationship for over 20 years, he still reached out on various occasions to build our relationship.

5. **My spouse** - Having a partner has also helped me in discovering a lot about myself and the world. Most especially during challenging times and by not dwelling on the hardship of the moment but by being prayerful which has really helped our marriage and it has also strengthened my character.

6. **Learning from mistakes** - I've made a few mistakes in the past and I have also taken time to reflect on them, I have moved on by learning from them and I have also found a better approach to dealing with situations. If we never make mistakes, we won't make anything at all. Failing once or several times doesn't make you a

failure but being afraid to take the risk means you will never get out of your comfort zone.

7. **Mindset** - Having a positive mind when everything else seems to be falling apart is worth being thankful for. If we tell ourselves that we don't have what it takes to stand out and be different or we don't have the strength to overcome our challenges, we would be letting ourselves down. We have to control our mindset because a healthy mind - free of negative thoughts will lead to a world full of light.

8. **Faith** - I chose to begin the hardest journey by living my life in a way that glorifies God in everything I do or say. Although the journey can be exhausting or testing, what has always kept me going is the belief and true faith in what God has in store for me and that it is greater than what I can ever imagine. Although it has been difficult because of the temptations but holding on to him and knowing that I have him as my best friend is worth being thankful for. My beliefs and values have given me a sense of purpose to stand for something much bigger than me.

9. **Ability to learn** - I create time to learn new things every day so I can develop the personal skills needed to do the things I love. After graduating from the university and while trying to secure a role in the wedding and events industry, I was told that I needed more practical experience. This was limiting my progress so I decided to attend trade shows, volunteer for event shows and attend seminars to acquire the required skills and refine my knowledge and as a result of that, I was able to establish a career in wedding planning. Therefore, learning is the stepping stone to acquiring other skills that can open you to greater opportunities.

10. **Life's challenges** - We have all experienced a slow pace of progress, hindrance in our journey but the major challenge is understanding why such delay happened. As you learn, you also grow to become a better version of yourself. It is through our setbacks that we exercise more faith, trust and hope. When you go through difficult times and decide not to give up, that is strength.

Your turn!

What are you thankful for? Take a few moments to think about this; you can use the following steps:

1) Identify 2 things that you appreciate about yourself. Choose meaningful things. These can involve your personality, your qualities, your actions, or anything else directly related to yourself.

2) Make a list of all the things you love and have. Once you've done that, cross out each item off the list, according to how least important it is and reflect on how you would feel if you were to lose them all?

3) Sometimes we tend to forget those who have helped us in one way or the other at a point in our lives and we do not reach out to them. Who, aside from family members, has helped you this month or in any way made you feel more comfortable about yourself?

4) Identify 3 people who have had a significant and positive impact in your life. These can be mentors, professors, bosses, family members, or anyone else. Remember them and think about how they have made an impact on your life.

10 Years from Now

How do you see yourself?

Where do you see yourself?

It's never too late to change your life

Conversation with Lawunmi Nwaiwu

10 Years from Now

I hope I'm still the same person I am now, just better

-   Lawunmi A Nwaiwu

The future is always a mystery and the funny thing is we never know what our future will be but we can only hope for the best. I have always had a passion for education. A passion to inspire and help others to achieve their potential through my work. I believe we can create the future that we so desire and it starts by creating it now. Some of us get so carried away thinking tomorrow is promised. Many of us are faced with daily decisions that can affect our future positively or negatively. The decisions we make today determine what lies ahead of us. We invest in today so that we can have a brighter tomorrow; one that even our future generations will look back and know we gave our best.

Honestly, sometimes when I think about life 10 years from now, it scares me a little because I have so many things I still want to achieve. I hope I can finally start doing most of the things I desire. One thing I am certain of is that God's plans supersede all of mine. If he gives me the opportunity to grow old, I want to have made the most of my present life and put all the talents he has given me into good use so I can change people's lives for better. As I continue to grow older, I hope to share my experiences, wisdom and perspective and also share what true faith has given me with the younger generation to come.

I hope to continue doing the things I love.

I want to have written many books that will not only educate people but also encourage them to make daily decisions that will turn their lives around positively and empower them to succeed.

Start thinking about the things you enjoy doing now. Many of us may feel that because we have not been able to accomplish our dreams years ago, the opportunity has gone but that's not true. Think of how badly you actually want the goal. You can achieve anything that you set your mind to do. I'm sure that with perseverance and with the help of the right people around you, you can live the life you've always dreamed of. Start today to create the life of your dreams. Start small, dream big and don't ever give up.

I hope to be a better me.

Well, that's the plan! If we are still in the same place for so many years, it means we are neither not moving forward nor backwards. Personally, as I grow, I want to be able to see a difference in me, from where I was to where I am now. If we continue doing the same thing we have been doing before, then we will keep arriving at the same destination. In the past, I was always distracted by the things going on in my life that I forgot to let the plans of God happen in its own way and time. I made that change to let him take full control of everything and direct me in his own way. For me to grow as an individual, certain things need to change - in my business, in my work, with those I meet, and with my environment and experience.

Living in the present for the future.

Living for the future is how we build many of our long-term goals and dreams. Living in the present and for the future are both equally important to me. Living today is about learning and developing ourselves, having awareness of our well-being and doing the things that bring purpose and also make a difference in our lives and that of others. Every day, we experience something new with the hope that tomorrow will be better. Most things that I have today didn't exist 10 years ago. Things have changed with innovations and development that we've had to adapt to, which has also changed our mindset. Don't get lost in time! Learn to stay ahead of change especially in tough times. If you have a business, do some research on your industry, find out what is new or changing, so you can drive your business or else you would be driven out of business.

Conversation with Lawunmi Nwaiwu

Q. 1   Tell me about a project or an accomplishment that you consider to be the most significant in your career?

A. 1   One of the projects I worked on was organising a family fun day fundraising event, which was used to support Africa Educational Trust to help build stronger education systems for all in the face of conflict and poverty in Africa. Working together as a team with other amazing event vendors, we were able to raise an amazing £491.25 to support education in Africa; giving people who missed out on school the chance to gain the skills and knowledge they want and need.

Q. 2   Why was it important to write this chapter - *10 years from now*? What does it mean to you?

A. 2   Imagining what I would like my life to look like starts from now - the present. I've learnt that life is not a book that you can write before you have lived and that is why the future is an ideal life I'd want to have, but I believe God's plans supersede all. Until then, look out for what's to come. More amazing books ahead as I continue my journey in life. Don't forget to follow me on all my social media platforms where I'll continue sharing inspiring stories about my journey, 10 years from now.

About Lawunmi A Nwaiwu

About the Author

Booking Opportunities

Connect with Lawunmi

Review this Book

Who is Lawunmi A Nwaiwu?

Lawunmi A Nwaiwu, also called Golden, is a UK based African Wedding Planner and a university graduate with a master's degree in International Business and Marketing. A lover of sports, good music, simple fashion and big earrings.

Over the years, Lawunmi has had the opportunity to write inspirational books. She is the author of '*Starting a Wedding Planning Career with Limited Funds*' and '*Secrets to a Work-Business Balance*' and has since continued to manage her career as an Author-preneur, mother and wife.

Booking Opportunities with Lawunmi

Lawunmi A Nwaiwu is passionate about transforming lives and inspiring the younger generation to break through the challenges and storms of life, to discover their untapped talents and build the courage and determination to succeed in life. She provides a clear and practical blueprint for personal success, drawn directly from her life experiences.

Let's Connect!

Kindly reach out if you're interested in having Lawunmi Nwaiwu speak at your event on topics like:

❖ Inspiring women

❖ Education

❖ Breakthroughs & transformations in life

Email:	info@lawunmianwaiwu.com
Website:	www.lawunmianwaiwu.com
Instagram:	@booksofgolden
	@goldenaisleweddings
Facebook:	Lawunmi A Nwaiwu

Review This Book

Were you inspired by this book? Then your review will be greatly appreciated. It will help to increase the credibility of this book and in turn inspire others. You can review this book on:

- Amazon
- Social Media platforms e.g. Instagram, Facebook, etc.
- Email

Other books by Lawunmi A Nwaiwu

❖ Starting a Wedding Planning Career with Limited Funds [2015]

❖ Secrets to a Work-Business Balance [2017]

www.ingramcontent.com/pod-product-compliance
Lightning Source LLC
Chambersburg PA
CBHW072007060426
42446CB00042B/2178